LIVING YOUR LIFE

by

Dr. Reg Barrett

P.O. Box 87305
HOUGHTON
2041

Also by Dr. Reg Barrett:
THE JOY OF LIVING
AS A MAN THINKS
THE SUPER MAN
HOW TO SUCCEED BY SETTING YOUR GOALS

First Printed 1987
Reprinted 1989

ISBN 0 620 129263

Printed and bound by CTP Book Printers, Cape

BD9823

CONTENTS

I do trust that the contents of this book
will help those who are searching
for greater understanding
in order to live a happier life

AUTHOR

Thanks are due to "YOUR FAMILY"
magazine for permission to print
this edition in book form.

1   There's no substitute for parents

With so many outside organisations devoted to child training and development these days—thousands of Parents are doubting their own importance. Of course a great number appear to be quite happy to surrender their role as Spiritual and Moral teachers.

I believe it is the parents' influence—that forms the child's character.

Schools cannot teach children to be honest when there are conflicting values in the home. The young watch father and mother react to a problem and how they deal with it.

In a survey in the United States, children were given the opportunity to mark their own examination papers. A group of children from well-to-do middle class homes were proved to have cheated far more than a group of reformed-school children. Why? Because in the wealthier homes, while Honesty was hardly discussed—Success was the main topic. The children had seen their parents tell lies to promote their own interests. Under this kind of attitude it is impossible for young people to know what is right or wrong.

I believe that when a child is handled with love and discipline he or she will feel secure and able to cope with life's challenges when they grow.

I would like to suggest that children from a young age begin to learn to make decisions. So again they will watch their parents doing likewise and follow by example. Children will not be able to deal with problems on their own unless they have had guidelines shown them by the parents' correct attitude to decision making.

Likewise as soon a possible let them partake in family discussions and be allowed to voice their own opinions without any form of ridicule from the rest of the family. Note the amazing growth of children when they are able to express themselves in their home environment.

I have counselled many young people from 6 years to 18 years of age and virtually without exception they have felt there was a total lack of communication in the family.

In our modern society I am convinced too little time is given to the children. Of course I generalise about this as many parents do relate to their family commitment.

John and Mary lived in a fashionable suburb of Cape Town. Both were highly respected, and John was a director of a group of companies. They had two children, a daughter named Mary, and a son, Ian. Mary was 14 and Ian was 11. Both the children were highly intelligent and above average at school.

On a particular Saturday, John and Mary were having dinner with friends in Constantia. During the dinner party, the telephone rang and the host asked if John could come to the 'phone. A well-wisher said that if they wished to assist their daughter they should go to a certain address in Bishops Court immediately. John could get no further information, and, rather perplexed, returned to the dinner table and asked if he and his wife could be excused. On arrival at this house, which appeared to be in complete darkness, John tried the front door, and it opened. In dim light he saw lots of young people caressing each other, and suddenly they saw their own daughter standing on the dining room table, completely nude, dancing. The mother fainted—the father, naturally, sent everybody home.

This is a true case history which happened in Cape Town some while ago, and the story was related to me by the parents. They could not understand why the daughter could do such a thing. When we all sat around a table together, it was found that every Saturday these parties had been going on, and the girl had always told the parents she was going to a friend's house. Further chats revealed that the mother was a keen bowler, and belonged to the local bowling club, and the father spent most of his time at business, and when he was not working was always out playing golf. Every Saturday evening, and on other such evenings, there were dinner parties and social get-togethers because of his business.

Mary, the daughter, told me that before she started these escapades, she wanted so much to be with her parents and go with them to the local cinema, or to one in town. Always, she said, it was "Next week, dear, your father and I are very busy. I'm sure you can look after yourself."

We, as parents, must realise that it is through us that the children are on this earth. Therefore, it is our responsibility to see that they are cared for in every way, and loved often. It must be remembered that a baby from the time it is born, can pick up the vibrations of the mother, and will know immediately when the mother is tense or unhappy. We tend to forget that children have the same mental capacity of thinking, accepting and rejecting, as we have as adults. Children are receptive to a smile, a hug and a kiss. We tend to forget that when we shrug them off they feel insecure, and they look to other avenues for this love.

In our modern society, when so many women have to, or

want to, go out to work, we find that the créche is now the new home. But inwardly the child is still needing the mother's love, and in so many cases it is found that the love given when the mother comes home, is really inadequate.

I was told the other day by a young mother that the bringing up of her two children was very boring, and that she could not wait very much longer before she found a nanny so that she could go out to business once more. With this statement, we should not wonder as the years go by that the parents are making a rod for their own backs, and the children who have been slighted and pushed aside are now outwardly revolting against the parents' behaviour of yesteryear.

Statistics here, in South Africa, are certainly none to be proud of. Our divorce rate gets higher and higher. The homes for retarded children become fuller and fuller, and the mental homes are filled with neurotics—and yet we read and hear it said that this is the result of our modern, fast way of living. In actual fact, it is basically the result of selfishness and immaturity from the adults' point of view. What kind of example are we setting when we say with one breath to a child "you must not do this, you must not swear, you must not behave like that," when we ourselves some half an hour later are doing and saying the same things for which the child has been punished? After all, the mother and father are always looked upon as the prince and princess of a child's dreams. Nothing they do or say can be wrong. They accept without question our beliefs, our way of living, our way of conducting ourselves in and out of home. They become part of a habit system, be it good or bad. And suddenly the prince and princess are fighting, and then there comes a separation, and the child has to choose between father and mother, and yet not live under the same roof. A weekend here, a weekend there, wondering what it is all about, being spoilt by both parents because of their guilt complex. And then we have the audacity to wonder why there are so many seeming delinquents!

Another case history is that of a young couple with two children who found, or believed, that their marriage was useless and that they were certainly incompatible. Both blamed the other one for the breakup, and, like so many such cases, the children were pushed aside, and it became a question of who had the car, who owned the house, who owned this and who got that, and eventually, and only at the end, was it decided who would take the children. In this particular case neither of them felt they wanted the children, and although the parents were young and healthy (in body only), the children found themselves, one aged 5 and the other aged 7 in an orphanage. Was it any wonder that the authorities inside the orphanage found that every night the younger child would scream and have nightmares? And whilst all this was going on, the mother and father were dividing the spoils.

Fortunately, in this particular case, the wonderful thing was that they both became more and more mature of thinking, and after a six month separation they found that they needed each other's love, and above all, missed the children. Today, this family is truly happy and have a further addition to the family. But with a lot more mature thinking on their part, so much misery could have been avoided.

In normal homes where family life continues under a satisfactory behaviour pattern, why have so many modern

5

parents become bewildered about their role? Probably it is because this modern approach has changed the pattern of family life. For centuries the family was a self-contained unit. Girls learned from their mothers how to cook and sew and boys learned from their fathers how to plant, hunt, build and defend the home. Along with these skills, children learned a set of goals in life and a concept of morality. But now, fathers work far from their sons and see them only during leisure hours. Mothers buy pre-cooked foods and ready-made clothing. Having lost the old techniques of child-rearing, we have certainly not found many new ones. This does not mean that the job is beyond the ability of modern parents, but it does mean that they must consciously lavish time and ingenuity on the job of child-rearing. As children get older let them become part of the unit insofar as to the choosing of furniture, the idea of decoration. Let us stimulate a little more enthusiasm inside our own homes, and this can be done, again, by the example of the parents.

There is a tendency these days for parents to put their children on pedestals. They must be good in everything they do. They must have special ballet lessons, tennis lessons, cricket coaching etc. They are always being held up as being the greatest when there is a discussion between friends. And yet, if we only realised that we were creating inside the child a feeling of being completely inadequate because he does not measure up to the desires and wishes of his parents!

Psychologists agree that a basic liking for people can be created or prevented during the child's first year of life. If an infant is always handled gently, fed when hungry, and comforted when miserable, it begins to get a fundamental trust in others and an unshakeable liking for human beings. Parents who are impatient, easily angered, or too busy to spend time with their children, are building characters with sand. It is the child's love of his parents that makes him want to adopt their best traits and learn the qualities they urge upon him. After all, to get happiness out of marriage, out of children, one has got to put back exactly what one takes out of it. If you want a highly successful, dynamic and wonderful home environment for your children, and yourself, then you have got to work for this. It does not come without the hard work that is necessary to achieve these ends, but the end result is really worthwhile.

2 *Overcoming shyness*

Shyness can almost always be conquered. The first step is to realize that it is not some quirk or a "put on" but is something that is very real and has to be dealt with and eventually overcome.

It is an uncomfortable state of mind and a somewhat immature one. For the sake of our social comfort and that of other people, we are well advised to change the state of mind. And once we have begun to treat the matter as a simple problem of growing up a little more, and not as some dramatically mysterious weakness, we are on the way to curing it.

Shyness is very much commoner than most shy people are aware. Almost everyone has at sometime had to fight against it, and people who outwardly appear enviably easy and confident are often people who have, earlier in life had exhausting battles against shyness and won the victory.

The shy person may safely assume that all kindly and intelligent people will feel at least some sympathy for an attempt to overcome shyness, and will be ready to help as far as their time and interest allow.

What about the people who do readily snub others? The people who are neither kindly nor understanding?

The answer to that, for the shy and timid person, can be a brutally plain one. The opinions of people who are neither kindly nor intelligent are worth nothing anyway. They are probably far more immature and ill-adjusted than the shy person they presume to scorn.

How can a shy person, male or female set about a

practical campaign to overcome this uncomfortable state of mind and gain confidence?

First, he or she must honestly want to do this: Must understand that we are members of the human race, need one another and are happier with a normal sexual, family and social life; must also understand that, just as he or she needs other people to be a complete and healthy personality, other people need him or her.

Everyone who is well-intentioned can fulfil some human need for some other person. It is on this basis of healthy principle and sensible acceptance of the nature of life that the shy person can begin to adjust his or her attitudes and behaviour.

Here are some of the more important mental techniques to aid the shy person.

1. *Cancel past discouragements*

Many people feel shy because of some mistake, punishment, humiliation or embarrassment in the past, sometimes in the remote past.

A small boy upsets the teapot at a birthday party and adults make this too big a catastrophe. He feels that he is clumsy and useless, and for years is secretly afraid, at any social event, that something similar will happen.

A girl of fifteen goes to a dance, and a boy of her own age, because he himself is shy and ill at ease, defends himself by saying something cruelly and stupidly rude to her. Too young to understand his own pathetic attempt to feel important. She is so much wounded that for years she cannot meet boys in a natural and happy way.

These mishaps do occur, and they do hurt people very

9

much. They are an important factor in really painful shyness.

Similarly, a person who has been too much rebuked or criticised, for example a child of strict parents, is apt to be very shy. When anything we say or do exposes us to the wounds of criticism or ridicule, it is not really surprising if we reach a point where we feel afraid to say or do anything.

Now the shy person who has been badly hurt can sink into self-pity and defeatism, resentment and morbid fearfulness. But he or she can also adopt this attitude: It was horrible; it was terrible; but it was in the past; throw it away—get rid of it!

Someone was unkind, hurtful, so what! Someone *was* but now have done with it—remembering all people are not that way.

Parents discouraged you and nothing you could do was right. O.K. face it—if nothing you could do was right, then your parents were wrong. They may have meant well, but fundamentally their judgments were incorrect and their demands unreasonable.

What matters is not the mistakes you once made, but the things you are going to do sensibly in the future. The shy person must take the attitude, things are going to be different from now on!

Remember that there is hardly a person on earth who has not, at sometime, been in a situation when he or she could have died of sheer humiliation. And remember there is no person on earth who has never made a mistake.

The seriously shy person must resolve: "I am not going to let it get me down, I am not going to be discouraged: I am worth more than the past would suggest; now for the future.

Mistakes are to be learned from. When we are hurt by some snub, criticism or insult, we can often help ourselves by thinking for a moment about the probable motives of the person who has hurt us. More often than not, we shall find jealousy, envy or a wish to be important as vital factors.

2. *Try to trust*

We become suspicious of one another at certain times, this is because we have all been badly let down at sometime.

Secret subconscious memories of past disappointments play a part in our feelings of mistrust or insecurity. Yet society is held together by bonds of mutual trust. Business relationships, marriage and friendships are all part of believing in others.

There are far more trustworthy people around, than the opposite. So now begin to trust yourself.

3. *Remember others are shy too*

One of the great troubles of the shy person is that everyone else seems to be so confident and at ease. This judgment is so often incorrect, as they too are only putting on a front—but within themselves they feel incompetent.

Shyness is nearly always cured if the shy person wants badly enough to help others. I have been involved in many such cases. When I have suggested joining a group to assist in helping others—the shy person says "Oh I couldn't do that". But after great effort they have offered to help the society which gives service to the less fortunate—the shy person begins to open up and learns that by serving others they overcome their own feelings of doubt.

So should you be shy, then make a plan to serve others as soon as possible. By forgetting yourself you help yourself overcome your challenge of shyness.

4. *Take care of personal appearance*

It is possible to worry far too much about ones appearance. "I am too fat or too thin." Instead of dressing according to ones feeling of assurance and confidence a shy person often develops "I couldn't care less attitude".

By taking an interest in ones appearance, self-confidence helps the shy person to be more aware of his or her ability.

One thing a shy person can do and that is to seek help in order to overcome this unhappy state of mind.

I have assisted many to change their attitudes and find a satisfactory answer to this nagging problem.

When you feel like a million dollars—you act like it.

5. *Take care of speech*

A really shy person is often helped by a course of speech training, or a course of "How to express oneself". This really does assist the timid person and instills self-confidence and self-respect. Another method is to use a cassette player and by listening to your own voice you pick up whether or not you are speaking too softly or stammering a little.

6. *Have something to say*

Many shy people can help themselves by reading and travelling—so that they can join in discussions and take part in stimulating conversation.

There is nothing worse than sitting silently at a gathering without saying a word and feeling totally inadequate.

At first it appears hard to get involved in conversation but one has to perservere until the shyness is overcome. After the first few times the effort to speak becomes easier and one is far more relaxed and has a feeling of being comfortable with others.

7. *Cultivate a sense of humour*

When we have a good sense of humour we are well on the way to overcoming shyness. Laughter brings happiness and is one of the greatest ways of feeling at ease in the company of other people. Make an effort to develop a sense of humour. A shy person soon loses his or her timidity when they take part in being happy and filled with joy and happiness.

8. *Remember that love is a master-key to life*

We must learn that love starts within ourselves, and this brings peace of mind, happiness and contentment. With this ever-abounding love, we can then give, give and give again. Allow love to vibrate throughout your family and home. Love brings unity and understanding in the home and in oneself. It is the very foundation of strength and courage. It is the greatest weapon in a crisis.

From the family unity, we turn to our attitude to our friends and colleagues. This is where the brotherly love is needed. At times it appears that we are not understood and feelings of resentment and hurt may creep in. At this stage we must take stock of ourselves and find out if we have slipped up. The hardest thing to do is to forgive the other person when on the surface we feel we are blameless. If we overcome this attitude of mind, then victory is ours. This is the true meaning of love—giving out when you expect nothing back. This way shyness has already left us — because loving is an outward-going experience and we are no longer thinking of ourselves.

If we achieve this then peace of mind will become a way of living and love will flow back towards you from many unexpected sources.

So we can see that when we spend time helping others we forget our shyness and become persons who enjoy living and happiness abounds.

> **A smile is the only thing in the world that you can't break by cracking**

3 *How to achieve a happy marriage*

PART ONE

In our modern western society it seems it is a miracle to find a really happy marriage. From the thousands of letters I have received over the last seven years—marriage is a convenient partnership. Much of the believed glamour is only a fantasy. But can it really work and be a glorious experience? I believe it can!

Looking back over 47 years of our marriage it has been exciting—active and certainly worthwhile in all aspects. I can see plainly that there are certain attitudes and practices which contribute to the success of any marriage.

1. *Don't expect perfection in your partner*

The more ardent the love of courtship days, the greater the possibility of being blind to any shortcomings in the beloved. In the glaring intimacy of married life, however, few blemishes of character can remain, for long, hidden. You may now say what about the idea of living together, a kind of trial marriage—without the total commitment, surely by this method we should see if we were compatible! Well let me tell you one story of many, where the trial run failed. In my book the super man I related this story.

Some while back a young couple came to see me about marriage. Let me call them Mary and John. They had lived together for some 18 months—both of them in their mid-twenties. This is how they expressed themselves to me. "We have tried out all the facts of what married life is all about. We feel the time has come to get married and prepare for the time when a child could be planned."

They appeared head over heels in love, holding hands as they left my office. So wedded they became.

Six months later two people arrived looking crest-fallen and certainly unhappy—yes it was Mary and John. Now let's look at their situation updated.

Instead of looking lovingly at each other, there was an outer appearance of hostility, especially from Mary. "What has gone wrong?" I asked—I hardly finished the question before the wife said "wrong? Everything. When we were single we slept together with nothing on—it was glorious, carefree, and we were both excitingly happy. On our honeymoon, the first night I got into bed with nothing on, but John was wearing pyjamas." What on earth is all this about? "Oh" said John, now that we are respectable people, don't you think it is right to be like other married people? "Well" said Mary, "This new attitude didn't turn me on. But that was not all, for now we quarrel over money. Whereas before we shared, and managed, and had money over for pleasure, now John was questioning me about what I spent on myself and food.

Whereas Mary was quite happy to carry on living as she did when out of wedlock, John felt protective and had developed in only six months a feeling of responsibility and respectability. When asked, John admitted he always used to wear pyjamas before he met Mary and, thinking to please her decided to discard them. About money, he felt they had to settle down in case a baby came.

Was he true to himself! It appeared as though he was not, as he wanted to please his girlfriend, but inwardly, or susconsciously, he really didn't approve. Old fashioned,

16

you may say. Yes, if you like, but deep race patterns are ingrained in our minds and will come to the surface from time to time. Funny how they seemed to enjoy each other before marrying and both were looking for the weaknesses and not seeing the good points.

Where did they fail—as in most activities there was no in-depth communication, no discussions about whether being married would change either of them in anyway.

Without complete understanding about what is expected of each other—even living together cannot be a mirror of what marriage is all about.

A BRIDE'S PRAYER

O Father, my heart is filled with a happiness so wonderful, I am almost afraid. This is my Wedding Day. I pray Thee that the beautiful joy of this day may never grow dim with tears of regret for the step I am about to take. Rather may its memories become more sweet and tender with each passing anniversary.

Thou hast sent me one who seems all worthy of my deepest regard. Grant unto me the power to keep him ever true and loving as now. May I prove indeed a helpmate, a sweetheart, a friend, a steadfast guiding star among all the temptations that beset this impulsive heart of mine.

Give me skill to make home the best loved place of all. Help me to make its light gleam brighter than any glow that would dim its radiance. Let me I pray Thee, meet the little misunderstandings and cares of life more bravely.

Be with me as I start my mission of womanhood, and stay Thou my path from failure all the way. Walk with us even unto the end of our journey.

O Father bless my wedding day. Hallow my marriage night. Sanctify my Motherhood if Thou seest fit to grant me that privilege.

And when all my youthful charms are gone and cares and lessons have left their traces, let physical fascination give way to the greatest charm of companionship.

And so may we walk hand in hand down the highway of the valley of the shadow which we hope to lighten with the sunshine of good and happy lives.

O Father this is my prayer. Hear me I beseech Thee.

Amen

2. *Recognise and meet sexual needs*

The fact that this is not often done accounts for many broken marriages. In my own analysis of the scores of letters regarding separation and even the reason for divorce, sex disagreement is one of the most outstanding causes.

Many a man goes into marriage thinking his wife will be as glamorous and seductive as the latest much publicized sex-kitten from Hollywood. In consequence there is much disappointment as far as the male is concerned and the wife feels totally inadequate. This important part in the unity of marriage should be fully discussed. Again with complete honesty.

I am of the opinion that classes should be held on marriage and what each expects of each other should be talked about openly. I have done many such classes and it is quite amazing how little each couple really knows how the other thinks.

What is needed is greater imagination—understanding patience and thoughtfulness.

3. *Appreciate emotional needs*

Both partners need to feel appreciated. It is doubtful

whether any marriage ever floundered where man and wife each realised this and not only showed appreciation of the other's qualities and achievements, but expressed that appreciation verbally.

We all long to be appreciated and we all delight in being praised. Husbands and wives should remember this and act accordingly to their partners.

Perhaps a woman's greatest need is to feel safe and secure. Not only an adequate regular income is required for this. She needs constant reassurance that she is loved—frequent reminders of her husband's affection.

Wives must realise that their husbands have needs other than sexual ones. They need prestige, to feel important. A wife can help to meet this need by the way she behaves to her husband and the things she says to him.

Both partners should appreciate the strength of the urge to create. Especially in a childless marriage should each encourage the other in some creative pursuit. No matter if it means a room being untidy or some hours of loneliness for the other; the partner who is creating something is generally easier to live with.

4. *Allow for differences in attitudes and abilities*

So often we expect our partner to agree with us in nearly all things, but this can and does cause deep hurt and later resentment. After all we married as individuals and although we live together we must respect the others points of view.

5. *Expect some snags and difficulties*

Modern marriage makes heavy demands. It insists that completely different personalities shall live amicably together for the rest of their lives.

The amazing thing is that this is so often achieved. Yet behind every successful marriage there must lie much patience, self-control and unselfishness to say nothing of many a row, much disillusionment and some heartbreak.

Those embarking on marriage are wise, therefore, to expect that although life with a loved one will have its times of bliss and be generally happy, there will be occasions when strong differences of opinion arise, accompanied sometimes by disappoinments, anger or tears.

There will be other snags, too, besides those arising from two different temperaments trying to live harmoniously together. There may well be difficulties with regard to accommodation, in-laws, careers, money, neighbours, children.

It is as well to develop an attitude that is prepared to meet difficulties in the marriage and handle them with courage, patience and fortitude.

6. *Develop a sense of humour*

There are times in married life when the ability to see the funny side of the situation is a great help. What looks like developing into a crisis can sometimes be rendered harmless by a laugh. Laughter is a great cleanser and assists in making the husband and wife more relaxed.

Even though we may not be able to laugh, a smile does so much to maintain harmonious relationships and gives victory over circumstances.

7. *Never attempt to dominate or restrict*

Men attempt to dominate their wives, and women attempt to restrict their husbands. These are two mistakes commonly made by married couples. Either attempt may meet with a measure of success but sometimes at heavy cost, namely the love of each other.

Old ideas live on surprisingly. Many a man still thinks that marriage gives him the right entirely to dominate his wife. She is, so he believes, no longer permitted to hold opinions different from his, to follow her own interests or to have any right to her own life.

Many a young wife resents her husband having time to spend on his sport or with his old friends.

Unless these inner conflicts are brought out into the open as soon as possible, problems will appear and in the end a feeling of rejection is felt by both husband and wife.

8. *Develop outside interests*

There is little doubt that it is wise for both parties to have a hobby or outside interest. Meeting other people is I believe a must as it gives man and woman a break from routine.

A husband should encourage his wife in such an interest though it may mean a lonely evening for him. His wife will return more alert, relaxed and happy as a result of her evening away.

A husband too will be more relaxed and reasonable if he sometimes has opportunities of mixing with people other than his colleagues, and if he has the satisfaction and distraction of pursuing an interest outside his work and home.

9. *Work at making marriage a success*

A happy and lasting marriage requires continual effort and attention. There must be the will on the part of both to make the union a success.

Herein lies the argument against trial marriages: when difficulties arise, there is not the effort to overcome them.

Working to make a marriage a success involves concentrating upon the successful and acceptable aspects of it, and making light of the reverse. It demands nurturing gratitude for past and present blessings rather than a hankering after the novel and unattainable.

Marital bliss is like a sensitive plant—it requires careful cultivation. It must be fed by thoughtfulness and consideration and supported by loyalty-trust and self-discipline.

In Part Two I will discuss further some of the problems we meet in marriage and how to solve them.

BEATITUDES FOR MARRIED COUPLES

Blessed are the husband and wife who continue to be affectionate, considerate and loving after the wedding bells have ceased ringing.

Blessed are the husband and wife who are as polite and courteous to one another as they are to their friends.

Blessed are they who have a sense of humour, for this attitude will be a handy shock absorber.

Blessed are they who love their mates more than any other person in the world, and who joyfully fulfill their marriage vow of a lifetime of fidelity and mutual helpfulness to each other.

Blessed are they who remember to thank God for their food before they partake of it, and who set aside some time each day for the reading of the Bible and prayer.

Blessed are they who attain parenthood, for children are a heritage of the Lord.

Blessed are the husband and wife who faithfully attend the worship service of a church for the advancement of God's Kingdom.

22

How to achieve a happy marriage

Blessed are the husband and wife who can work out their problems and adjustment without interference from relatives.

Blessed are they who have a complete understanding about financial matters and who have worked out perfect partnership with all the money under control of both.

Blessed are the husband and wife who humbly dedicate their lives and their home to God and practice the teaching of God in their home by being unselfish, loyal and loving.

TRIBUTE

I love you not only for what you are, But for what I am when I am with you. I love you not only for what you have made of yourself, but for what you are making of me. I love you for the part of me that you bring out.

I love you for putting your hand into my heaped-up heart, and passing over all the foolish and frivolous and weak things which you cannot help dimly seeing there, and for drawing out into the light all the beautiful, radiant belongings, that no one else had looked quite far enough to find.

I love you for ignoring the possibilities of the fool and the weakling in me, and for laying firm hold on the possibilities of good in me. I love you for closing your eyes to the discords in me, and for adding to the music in me for worshipful listening.

I love you because you are helping me to make the lumber of my life not into a tavern, but a temple, and of the words of my everyday not a reproach but a song.

I love you because you have done more than any creed could have done to make me good, and more than any fate could have done to make me happy. You have done it just by being yourself. Perhaps that is what being a wife means after all.

Anonymous

4 *How to achieve a happy marriage*

PART TWO

Someone once said "It doesn't matter much when you marry, because when you are married, you find you have married someone else." There is cynicism here, but also an element of wisdom.

Many of the snags of married life arise from three factors: (a) immaturity; (b) ignorance; and (c) intolerance. Let us look at each of these in turn.

(a) *Immaturity*

The failure of marriage often has its real cause in immaturity in at least one of the partners. He or she looks for perfection in the adored one, only to find that the prince or princess has feet of clay. Or one partner looks for some ideal of sexual satisfaction that can never be found. And why? Because he or she has not realised that either is immature.

A woman once said to me, there is only one thing I want of life, that is marriage. "Why I asked her".

"Because I want to be loved," she said.

But the desire to be loved, although healthy as far as it goes, is a very shaky foundation for marriage. There are really three stages in the growth of human love. The first is the desire to be loved. It is baby love.

The next stage is typical of courtship. It means "I love you because you are completely lovable". This is a wonderful experience.

But the mature love in which a true marriage blossoms

means something like this "I love you for what you are, and in spite of what you are. It involves the responsibility of keeping on loving when things go wrong. Such love grows on its difficulties and becomes deeper and richer with the years. If you can learn to love like that, there will be no breakdown in your marriage.

(b) *Ignorance*

Marriage is a grown-up business, not a frolic for children. To go into marriage with confidence, you need to know not only the normal facts of life and sex, but something of the arts of married courtship.

It is quite amazing the number of letters sent to me relating to the lack of knowledge what marriage is all about. To be successful at any profession or trade we have to study and learn all we can before we can master the job on hand. Hours, weeks—months and years are spent to accomplish this. Not so with marriage, little, if no effort is put in to discover what living together as a married couple really requires. It is a hit and miss affair.

But let us be strictly honest "what has been my motives to marry" Let me tell you a few reasons for marriage, that I have been told either by letter or in a personal interview.

1. *From a woman's point of view.*

   To father my child: Born out of wedlock.
   To have my own place.
   To make my own decisions.
   To move out of an unhappy environment.
   To have security.
   To be needed.

Of course there are many more—but note not one of the above gives any suggestion of giving out love and sharing life with the man of her dreams.

2. *From a man's point of view.*
   To be taken care of.
   To have sex without looking for it.
   To feel needed.
   To run a home efficiently.
   To move out of an unhappy environment.

Again many more can be added—but no mention of giving out love and sharing joy and happiness.

A man sometimes wishes to compare his wife to his mother and desires that the wife gives him the same kind of consideration as the mother. This can be a disastrous situation—because women today in general will not accept this. Nor is it right for them to do so. There is the following poem which is highly amusing.

NOTHING SUITED HIM

He sat at the dinner table there, with a discontented frown,
The potatoes and steak were underdone and the bread was baked too brown.
The pie was sour, the pudding too sweet, and the mincemeat much too fat.
The soup was greasy too and salty, 'twas hardly fit for a cat.

"I wish you could taste the bread and pies I have seen my mother make.
They were something great, and 'twould do you good just to look at a slice of her cake."

Said the smiling wife "I'll improve with age, just now I'm only a beginner,

How to achieve a happy marriage

But your mother called to see me today and I got her to cook the dinner.

Author unknown

"Makes you think doesn't it"

How to say goodbye in the morning

Are you the romantic type of man who wants his wife up in the morning looking fresh (after a good night's rest)? Do you feel that this will put you on the right path for the day? Well, if she doesn't do this, have you asked her? All of us are creatures of habit. We get into a particular groove and stay there until something is changed.

I really believe that a family should all sit down to breakfast together every morning, where possible of course. It is a happy man who sees his wife and children before taking off for work. It gives a solid foundation to the start of a day.

Years ago when we were living in an apartment, I used to leave early in the morning and I watched with interest the early morning reaction to parents taking their children to school. Some were happily going together, mother and father leaving for business and taking children to school—others rushing, out of sorts, literally dragging their children and roughly putting them in the car—some with tears, others shouting and mummy and daddy "doing their nut" as one father told me. What a start to a day.

"Yes" you could say, "are you not trying to make life look like cloud nine with everyday a smile and no upset at all?" Of course there are days when things do go wrong. But we should really try to cope most of the time.

Even without children, I have seen couples barely saying a goodbye to each other in the mornings.

I repeat that the early morning period can be a glorious relationship of communication—that is, if both husband and wife decide to make it so.

(c) *Intolerance*

Marriage involves the distinct personalities with different upbringings, traditions, family customs, habits and attitudes to life. These two different personalities are hoping to stick together for the rest of their lives. Some of the things you think absolutely essential to a happy life, your partner may consider irrelevant or even harmful.

It is only when you are married that you realise what differences of conviction exist. If you are intolerant and dictatorial you may win your point, but you may, in time, lose the respect of your partner. When respect has gone, love eventually goes too.

What then are the foundations of a happy married life? I would like to mention three.

First

Foster a growing love-relationship in which both partners take equal but diverse responsibilities.

Second

See to it that there is as much self-expression for each partner as is possible.

Third

Keep the intimate side of married life a fresh and growing experience.

So may be the following could be of assistance.

28

THE ART OF MARRIAGE

Happiness in marriage is not something that just happens. A good marriage must be created. In the art of marriage the little things are the big things.

It is never being too old to hold hands.

It is remembering to say "I love you" at least once a day.

It is never going to sleep angry.

It is forming a circle of love that gathers in the whole family.

It is at no time taking the other for granted. The courtship shouldn't end with the honeymoon, it should continue through all the years.

It is doing things for each other, not in the attitude or duty or sacrifice, but in the spirit of joy.

It is speaking words of appreciation and demonstrating gratitude in thoughtful ways.

It is not expecting the husband to wear a halo or the wife to have the wings of an angel. It is not looking for perfection in each other. It is cultivating flexibility, patience, understanding and a sense of humour.

It is having the capacity to forgive and forget.

It is giving each other an atmosphere in which each can grow.

It is finding room for the things of the spirit. It is a common search for the good and beautiful.

It is not only marrying the right partner, it is being the right partner.

It is discovering what marriage can be, at its best, as expressed in the words Mark Twain used in a tribute to his wife: "Wherever she was, there was Eden."

5 *The leaders of tomorrow*

I believe most sincerely in the youth of today. They will not start a task without asking why do I have to do this.

The cry of youth is for life! More life! The purpose of this article is to encourage, inspire and stimulate boys and girls who long to be somebody and do something in the world. But feel that they have little chance in life.

The biggest room in the world is the room for self-improvement.

Let us look at a few facts that can change a life of doubt or fear to successful achievement.

(a) *Self-reliance*

Of all the elements of success, none is more vital than self-reliance—a determination to be one's own helper and not to rely on others for support. This does not mean that we do not learn from others—for this is important, but it does mean you have to get stuck in and do the work by your own effort.

For those of you who have seen the movie "Chariots of Fire" will remember the two major roles—those of Harold Abrahams the winner of the 100 metres at the 1924 Olympic Games and that of Eric Liddell.

I was trained by Harold Abrahams to run the 100 yards and the 220 yards. He was a hard coach but his methods and instructions were outstanding. He told me, I can show you how and what to do "but you have got to do it." My own successes can be attributed to his coaching and my own desire to win.

30

So learn well but rely on your own ability to succeed.

(b) *Mental attitude*

There is nothing so important in your life as your mental attitude towards yourself, what you think of yourself. The model which you hold of yourself and your possibilities.

I wish it were possible to impress upon the minds of the young the tremendous power which right thinking can do to bring about success. Convictions that you are meant to succeed. The truest way to aid the body, the surest method by which abnormal, physical or moral conditions can be overcome, is through mental development, by getting the mind right. By creating the right atmosphere within, by enlarging the mental horizon of your life. In this way only can the highest results be attained.

To get your thinking right and your fears and doubts will leave you.

(c) *Setting your goals*

It is astonishing how many people there are who have no definite aim or ambition, but just exist from one day to another with no well-defined life plan.

All about us are the future citizens aimlessly drifting without any idea of what they intend to do after school or college.

It is not enough for success to have ability, education, and health. Thousands have all these and still fail because of their attitude to successful achievement. Their ability is placed at a disadvantage by the lack of a big motive.

Become an individual and leave your mark on the world.

Your definite aim in life should be selected with deliberate care, and after it has been selected it should be written out and placed where you will see it at least once a day. The reason for this, is that each time you read it, the effect is imprinted on your subconscious mind so strongly that it accepts it without question. Eventually you will automatically speak about your burning desire in your day to day activities. Finally you will do that which you desired as a matter of course.

But what about the young person who cannot find the path to follow, how can he or she get to grips with this problem!

I suggest you try the following method which could help find the solution.

List on a piece of paper all the professions and business ventures you can think of. Take time to prepare this. Then before you start to cross off the careers which you don't fancy, find out all you can about each one.

For example a young man aged 16 years was keen to become an accountant. After he had visited me about his career and his desire to become an accountant, I explained the length of time required for study, the serving of articles and attending university. I further suggested that during the summer school vacation he should ask a firm of accountants if he could attend their office daily and find out whether he had the feeling for the profession. He told me it gave him a fantastic insight to accountancy, but decided it was not for him. You see he learned about this "by going to find out for himself." A positive attitude. Otherwise he could have chosen the wrong career and wasted a year or two of his young life. I have suggested to many young people to find out all they can before embarking on a career. Otherwise there are many, disallusioned boys and girls, extremely unhappy about their futures.

When you have acquired all the necessary information both in theory and practice you are ready to set your goals.

There should be at all times small goals—leading up to the ultimate one. For example let us presume you are in Standard 8 at school. The first goal is to pass your examinations in order to be promoted to Standard 9.

So I suggest you write out several goals until you reach the one you really desire. Rather like this.

Goal 1 Finish Standard 8
Goal 2 Complete Standard 9
Goal 3 Pass Matriculation
Goal 4 University B.A. B.Sc. or whatever
Goal 5 Receive university degree
Goal 6 Take your place in business–industry or commerce or profession.

Thomas Huxley wrote

The rung of a ladder was never meant to rest upon, but only to hold a man's foot long enough to enable him to put the other somewhat higher.

Unless you set positive goals you will become depressed and unhappy, because there is no purpose in your life.

(d) *Resolute determination*

I wrote in my book "How to Succeed by Setting your Goals"—the following thoughts:

(1) *Draw up daily–weekly–monthly and yearly schedules.* This will help you to master the study programme and help

to relieve the pressure which you place upon yourself for leaving everything until the last minute.

(2) *Give yourself a challenge.* If you give yourself a challenge you are more likely to accomplish all you would like to do. Say to yourself something like this, "This may be difficult, and it may be hard to complete what I have in mind for today, but I am going to prove I can do it."

Once you resolve that you are going to do this, it appears as though there is something that is pushing you on swiftly from one task to the next.

(3) *Maintain the "I can" attitude.* Nothing slows us down more than if we lack interest in whatever it is we are doing. When you say I can't do it—then cross off the "'t" from can't and you will now say "I can do it". When you do this you will surprise yourself by what you can accomplish.

(4) *Be regular.* It is imperative that you become regular in your habits in exactly the same way that you are regular in your day-to-day hygiene habits. If your minds are used creatively and correctly with the right resolute determination, then you will recognize that there are few formidable tasks which will not eventually yield to steady persistence effort.

To be spasmodic or irregular is asking for discouragement and defeat.

Regular persistent effort even though little is done at any one session, soon leads to results being seen and results measured.

In the art of studying, it is the persistency of seeing the task through to conclusion whatever it may be. You will soon find how successful you are.

(5) *A career based upon self-expression.* Put your whole self in whatever it is you have to do and you will find the end result is your self-expression.

Your career must be based on this, for there is no enjoyment, satisfaction or feeling of fulfillment if you do not express your own desires.

(e) *Get to grips with your family*

As a young person do you sometimes find it difficult to understand your parents. Why not try to solve this by going out of your way to find out how they tick. By this I mean see what they do each day. Make a plan to ascertain their needs. Because you are busy and your parents also busy little time is found to promote true friendship in the home. If the son is a friend of his dad and the daughter close to mum that is great. But mostly I have seen the parent–children association somewhat lacking in understanding.

I read the following which could assist you in getting close to your father.

"The other night a stock-broker friend of mine got to talking about his son Jack, who is a senior in high school. Last summer the boy wanted a car more than anything else in life, and my friend told him to get a job to earn the money for it. As it turned out his own brokerage firm needed extra help in the post dept. So Jack went to work there for the summer. He really was not very excited about the whole idea, but he had set his mind on a car! After a few weeks, his father asked him how he liked working, and Jack's reply was "Well Dad, I am certainly going to do something better with my life than just grubbing for money. It's all right for one summer, but for a lifetime . . . never!"

Living your life

One day on his rounds to collect the post, Jack fell into conversation with a young management trainee who was probably only four or five years older than Jack himself. The young man said to Jack, "Gosh you're lucky to have a man like Mr Field for a father. I came to work here because he's got a reputation for really taking the time to teach younger men the ins and outs. What a man!"

As the weeks went by Jack met other people in the company who told him similar stories about his father and how he helped young men and guided them. Finally one day Jack said to his dad "You know, you've been doing a lot of things behind my back all these years. I thought you went downtown every morning, made a lot of sharp deals, counted your money and called that living. It turns out you've really helped a lot of people."

His father said "Well Jack, I've actually spent my life doing what I wanted to do. I absolutely love my business. I determined to make my company a safe, comfortable, secure place people would be proud to work in. You can't change the whole world, Jack, but you can make your own part of it the way you want it to be. And I only hope that you find something to do with your life that captures your interest as my business has captured mine."

Jack learned a lot last summer, about his father and about himself.

You see how little we know about one another in the same family.

A young person would do very well and help the parent..youth situation if he were to think of his parents not as parents, but as people. Think of your mother not as a mother, but as a women, of your father, not as a father, but as a man. Having removed the emotional element you can now deal with these older people as you would with any human being, for as a human being they have reactions and feelings, the same as you have.

It might just be that we all can get together more surely with a person than with a parent. So a solution of the matter might be that parents treat their children as persons and not children and children treat their parents as persons and not parents.

One of the best ways in which a family can erase a gap, or for that matter prevent its appearance in the first place, is to act together as a team.

Parents should be the kind of people that kids can gripe with and not about. Shock reaction should never be allowed. One of the chief skills in human relations is to take every person as he is and accept him that way.

And again it must be remembered that every individual longs to be a person, his own person. Children should let parents be their own persons and accept them for what they are. And parents, should never think of their children as something they own or an expression of themselves.

Have a family of this order and any gap will shrink to a nothing.

So let us summarize this article

(a) You must believe in yourself and have self-reliance.
(b) Mental attitude towards yourself and others.
(c) Set your goals by planning and a positive mental attitude.
(d) Have a resolute determination to achieve success.

(e) Get to grips with your family. So vital for a happy successful life.

Nothing succeeds like success.

---

6 *Improving your life by positive thinking*

Positive thinking! Some people turn their noses up at it. Some are transformed by it. Some are cynical. Others depend on it as if it were a lifeline.

Some people say it has made all the difference in life to them. Others sneer at it as just another passing craze.

What is positive thinking? How does it work and what has it to give us?

Positive thinking is a practical technique in the art of living.

Why is positive thinking so important? The answer to this question is: Because it works on two psychological principles of basic importance to human nature.

(a) You can only get rid of a wrong idea or complex of emotions as you put a right one in its place.

(b) as Karl Menninger says: "Attitudes are more important than facts."

Let us look at these two vital principles.

(a) The right way to be rid of a wrong idea or complex of ideas is to replace it in mind by something that is positive and right. When you come to think of it, this is one of the simple commonsense ideas we can use as a daily exercise.

WRONG THINKING

If you think about it, you will recognise that many of us are chained to wrong systems of thinking. These wrong systems of thinking are permanent habits of mind.

We do not think them out. They are with us before we know it. They create reactions in our mind so that we find

Living your life

ourselves in a vicious circle of negative and destructive thinking.

They are triggered off by subconscious patterns deep within us. As a result, without our conscious awareness, many of us are allowing our great energies of mind to be wasted on thoughts and emotions of guilt, shame, misfortune, defeatism.

These thoughts of tragedy, worry, anxiety, shame and hopelessness come up from the subconscious mind, and we appear to be at their mercy. If we try to get rid of them without putting something else in their place, they will come again and again. The only hope of emerging into freedom comes from replacing these negative thoughts with something that is positive and dynamic.

A woman I know was almost in a broken-down state. She was over sixty, had no relatives to speak of, and she was trying to earn a little money by looking after an old selfish woman. Her employer's constant complaining brought her to breaking point.

Throughout the day, this helper's mind would revert to the hurts she received. She found herself at the mercy of a chain of thought that was depressing and hopeless. Her health was running downhill and she was completely at a loss.

One of her most vital needs was to replace her negative feelings and her hurtful thoughts with ideas that were positive, heartening, warm and cheerful.

I suggested to her this formula to repeat "Whenever I tend to feel resentful and to nurse grievences, that it is the signal to me to put my thought energies instead in an assurance of my value, in happy and positive thoughts, and to enjoy all the goodness of life."

40

I told her that whenever she found the poisonous thoughts running through her mind, she should repeat this formula.

Two weeks later I saw her again. She looked a different woman. Her eyes were bright, her footstep was stronger, and her face full of smiles. Her energy was renewed. "Your formula is wonderful" she said. "I feel a different person. My hope has returned."

Surely the right way to be rid of a wrong idea is to replace it in the mind by something that is positively right.

RIGHT ATTITUDE

(b) Attitudes determine our lives and if positive we can have a dynamic future.

Attitudes to life, to ourselves, and others play such an important role we should carefully watch what we think and how we think.

Are we cynical and disillusioned about life? Do we sum people up in our minds, always running them down? This is negative thinking. It is poison! It is a habit of mind that is doing us great harm. It is defeating our wholesome destiny.

But this position can be changed as we resolutely allow all these unworthy thoughts to be replaced by ones that are kind, understanding and loving.

Many walk through life carrying a perpetual sense of shame or guilt about something in our past. Remember the past has gone, the future is but a dream—so I can only live one day at a time, the "new" day.

It is necessary for us to remember the Almighty loves us

and forgives us all that we may have done wrong. It is also necessary for us to forgive ourselves. Then we can start again and go forward into life with self-assurance and greater confidence.

NOW BEGIN TO USE YOUR IMAGINATION

The imagination is a key by which we can grow and expand in the whole of our life, with all its challenges and sometime its disappointments.

Ask yourself as you read this article "Am I a truly happy person?" Do I wake up in the morning keen to get started on a new day? Do I as I dress, imagine some of the happy things I will achieve today? These questions are vital to you! If you can say with conviction—yes! I am a go-getter, a normally happy person—then you are making your path a pretty good one on which to walk. But! If the opposite is the case then begin to use positive imagination. By filling your subconscious mind with happy-prosperous thoughts eventually the old negative habits disappear and positive habits take over.

I have found personally to programme my subconscious mind just before going to sleep. I first of all look back on the day just finishing and make sure I have tried to do my best. Then if I have been rude or unkind to anyone I ask in prayer for forgiveness. Then I make up my mind I will not make the same mistake or mistakes tomorrow. Then I give thanks for all the happiness—joy and love I have received. Finally I now make the following statement.

As I go to sleep, I will know that I am preparing myself for a new day to come. I declare that I will awaken—

fresh—vital and filled with love. My new day will be a great day.

You will be surprised what takes place in your subconscious mind when you prepare yourself for success and happiness.

Maybe the following could help you!

Take time for work, it is the price of success.
Take time to think, it is the source of power.
Take time to play, it is the secret of youth.
Take time to read, it is the foundation of wisdom.
Take time to be friendly, it is the road to happiness.
Take time to dream, it is hitching your wagon to a star.
Take time to love, it is the highest joy of life.
Take time to laugh, it is the music of the soul.

All these thoughts are positive ones, each in turn will add greatness to you! Try to put them all into action and watch a person of fantastic vitality emerge.

ENTHUSIASM

Without enthusiasm we cannot reach the heights we were meant to. So many have great ability but few have the enthusiasm that sets the wheels into motion.

Walter Chrysler once said . . .

"The real secret of success is enthusiasm.
Yes, more than enthusiasm.
I would say excitement.
I like to see men excited.
When they get excited they make a success of their lives.
You can do anything if you have enthusiasm.
Enthusiasm is the yeast that makes your hope rise to the stars.

43

Enthusiam is the sparkle in your eye, it is the swing in your gait, the grip of your hand, the irresistible surge of your will and your energy to execute your ideas. Enthusiasts are fighters.

They have fortitude, they have staying qualities.

Enthusiasm is at the bottom of all progress.

With it there is accomplishment.

Without it there are only alibis"

There is, perhaps, no mistake of a young person more common than that of supposing that, in the pursuits of life, extraordinary talents are necessary to one who would achieve more than ordinary success. There is no greater genius than the genius of enthusiasm. It wins the prizes of life, which appeared destined to fall to those brilliantly constituted minds, who to some observers, seemed to be favoured by life. But they lacked enthusiasm, and in that want lacked all. Enthusiasm, with a moderate degree of wisdom, will carry a person farther than any amount of intellect without it. It gives them force and momentum. It is the active power of character, and if combined with self-assurance, will enable the person to employ their power to the best advantage in all the affairs of life.

It is the person although with limited academic knowledge, but impelled by enthusiasm who accomplish such magnificent results.

What is needed in South Africa at this very moment are people who with their vital energy can turn the nation into positive thinkers and success planners.

It is a Spanish proverb that says, "He who loseth wealth loseth much. He who loseth a friend loseth more; but he who loseth energy loseth all."

Maybe the following thoughts will open up new horizons for some and maybe light a fire under many.

44

"The man who feels no enthusiasm for his work will never accomplish anything worthwhile"   Sir William C. Van Horne.

Enthusiam will open a door when other keys fail.

Enthusiasm is the compelling power that overcomes all difficulties.

"A smile is the only thing in the world that you can't break by cracking."

Dr Norman Vincent Peale—the father of "Positive Thinking" writes as follows:

"A physician remarked that about half of the people who come into his office do not actually have anything physically wrong—they've just had the life knocked out of them and as a result have become prey to worries and fears. He said if only he could go to a shelf, get down a good bottle of enthusiasm, and inject a little of it into the bloodstream of these patients, he could restore their health and vitality. Fear and enthusiasm never mix."

So from now on try to be positive in all you do and you will suddenly feel a new person filled with vitality and joy.

7 *How to alter your way of life*

Many people feel that they are not getting what they should out of life.

"I am dissatisfied" Said a man to me. I have reached thirty years of age and have got exactly nowhere".

"The years are slipping by" Said a girl. But neither marriage nor happiness has come my way.

Our fulfilments do not accord with our dreams. Life has become a second best. We hoped once to be successful but find ourselves the odd person out, full of fears and worries and hesitation.

How can we help ourselves to make a success of the greatest concern in all the world—THE BUSINESS OF LIVING?

From the encouragement I have received in my own experience, and from years of helping people, I want to suggest four simple steps that we can all take, with a view to transforming our life from Colourlessness to Radiance and from Failure to Success.

1. *Cultivate belief in yourself*

Of all necessities that make for a happy and worthwhile life; Belief in oneself is the greatest essential.

"As a Man Thinketh, So is He". Said king Soloman.

If we drag ourselves through each day with a sense of uselessness-guilt—no purpose—it is impossible for us to enter into Freedom, Enjoyment and Reward that Life can yield us.

46

If, for any reason, you are burdened with guilty feelings about yourself and tend to run yourself down as worthless, know that there can be a change in you right away. If you go around with a perpetual feeling of guilt, then you can get rid of it by doing three things.

Receive the forgiveness of the Almighty. (For He is Love and Delights to Forgive.) Show a forgiving spirit to those who have wronged you.

Above all, forgive yourself. Reinstate yourself in your own esteem and know that whatever life has been in the past, it can be different now.

A little while ago a girl told me, with considerable humiliation, of an unfortunate episode that had spoilt her life years ago. She was still carrying around the burden and shame of it.

I had to show her that only as she forgave herself as a worthwhile member of society, leaving the past behind, could she know happiness—freedom—poise and enjoyment.

We must believe in ourselves and in our destiny and we must cultivate this belief everyday. A very good way to encourage ourselves is to repeat this little sentence with sincerity, conviction and with deep feeling, every morning, if possible, just as we wake up:

"WHENEVER I FEEL WORTHLESS, THAT IS THE SIGNAL TO KNOW I AM ACCEPTABLE AND I SHALL MAKE A SUCCESS OF MY LIFE THIS DAY".

Our life is what our thoughts make of if.
'Marcus Aurelius'

---

2. *Discover the rewards of discipline*

Discipline can be great fun. Many people make the mistake of forcing themselves into a kind of negative attitude in order to believe that discipline to find success is a bind.

After a few days they suddenly collapse with discipline in pieces.

The way to make personal discipline successful is to use, not will power, but vision and imagination. We need to map out the way we wish to go and have a clear view of it in mind.

We need to feel a thrill of excitement in fixing a reasonable target for our efforts and have a sense of warmth in the achievement that is going to be ours.

As we keep this vision burning brightly and see ourselves as the sort of person who is really accomplishing it, our exercises in Discipline become happy adventures.

Many of us are troubled with that age long bugbear of secret laziness. "Oh, I can't be bothered" is what we feel.

The longer we stay in this rut of behaviour the more tedious it is to break the habit.

It is good for us to think constructively. If a thing is worth doing, it is worth doing well. We can put this kind of thought for every hour of the day.

With vision and discipline the day can be transformed. We must start the day well. We can plan our day so that it is lived to its maximum.

3. *Throw away self pity*

What is our worst enemy? There are numerous thoughts

on this subject. But I personally believe that self-pity is near the top of the negative parade.

Self-pity has wrecked more lives than most illnesses.

Self-pity edges its way into our secret thinking in such a subtle way, that before we know where we are, we are indulging in a whole pattern of negative thinking and of feeling sorry for ourselves.

Self-pity uses up so much of our energy that there is little left for a truly inspired and successful life. It is so easy to get into the habit of blaming others should any difficulty or misfortune enter our lives.

When we have exhausted all the sources of the blame— we even accuse fate of being against us. These excuses are all avenues that lead to self-pity.

It can be a turning point in our lives as we realise that for a number of years, self-pity has been our secret home and that without consciously realising it we have sub-consciously preferred the misery and hopelessness rather than going on our way to success and happiness.

A man who came to see me for counselling suddenly woke up to this facet of himself. He said: "I feel ashamed. I have been making excuses for myself and even sobbing like a child. I have been running away from reality. It has been self-pity and I recognise now, how I have enjoyed it all the way along. If life was not a bed of roses for me, I kicked and screamed in my alleged suffering".

How many of us would be brought to the same recognition if we looked deeply into ourselves?

Why do we stick to the secret gratification of self-pity? For two reasons.

(1) There is an underground element of satisfaction in it.

(2)   We fear to go forward into success, happiness and
      love, because these are lovely gifts of life that evaded
      us as infants. They are experiences that we have never
      really known or enjoyed and we are afraid of the
      unknown.

The way out of this dilemma is to discard the poor
gratifications of self-pity and to put our energies deliber-
ately into the adventure of the unknown.

We cannot have self-pity and at the same time enjoy
happiness and success. But if we put our imagination and
our basic energies into happiness and fulfilment, rather
than into bitter frustrations, we cannot fail to win through.

4.   *Practice being a warm personality*

It is natural for a little child to think in terms of "I
Want", but unfortunately many of us subconsciously have
grown up without changing that attitude to one more
suitable to adult years and social needs.

Our inner self is still hungering in a childish way, and
without awareness we are missing the adult thrills that
come from taking an initiative in warmth and friendliness.

Experience proves that more happiness comes to us in
what we give than in what we get and the thrill of coping
with our human situation successfully without being ruffled
ourselves, and the excitement of making those in our
immediate circle happy and comfortable, brings more
satisfaction in the long run than winning even a sweepstake
or the like.

If you feel starved of love, of encouragement and happiness, then it is good to recognise that other people feel
exactly the same. If one recognises this need in other

people, and give love and encouragement to them, the satisfaction rebounds like a boomerang upon oneself.

As we persevere with imagination into the experiment, we shall come to an enjoyment of life and a sense of well being and accomplishment such as we have never known before.

Keep out undesirable thoughts. The best way to do this is to keep the mind busy with vivid mental pictures of pleasant things, and of yourself doing the important things you wish to do in life.

In other words, a mind full of desirable thoughts leaves no room for any other kind.

D. Carlson.

8 *How to develop your concentration*

Concentration is a very large part of success in any task, whether it be making a sponge cake, playing tennis, preparing for an examination or organising an outing.

The secret of concentration, however, is no secret. Most of the rules are very obvious and simple. They are: take an interest; make an effort; remove distractions; relax.

It is also possible to improve our powers of concentration by special exercises. But the person who is already desperately busy and on the verge of panic can hardly sit down to mental exercises.

It will help to look at these rules more closely.

(1) Take an interest: "Chris!" the teacher scolds. "You are looking out of the window again. You must learn to concentrate."

The real trouble is that Chris is concentrating; he is concentrating with great attention on how the workmen across the road are preparing the underground pipes. He is most interested; he notices every detail; he cannot take his eyes off the proceedings.

The teacher however wants him to concentrate on how to deal with a maths problem. But this to Chris is boring to say the least.

A baby shows marvellous powers of concentration, often more than adults. A considerable part of bringing up a child seems to consist of interrupting its interest in something, because the parent wants the child to do something else. We know it is not too difficult to concentrate on the subject that interests us.

The problem of concentrating on a task is very largely the problem of how to produce some interest in it. The technique for this will vary, depending on the task. The best kind of interest is the one that stirs our emotions. However life does not consist entirely of tasks we really want to do. Many of them are not exciting and some extremely tiresome.

Here are a few possible techniques for bringing to a dull task enough interest at least to get it done as speedily and well as possible.

(a) *"This must be done; so let's get it over!"*

The sooner we have done a dull task properly, the sooner the thing is out of the way. It may be a help to say, when this is done, I will do something more interesting.

A young teacher had a class of very lazy, frivolous girls, who did not want to do their cookery lessons, and still more had no inclination to clear up afterwards. They seemed to be interested in nothing but make-up and clothes. The teacher, after a few failures, tried the following one day:

"Look; I have brought some different cosmetics in this box. If today you can do all your cooking and all the clearing-up properly before half-past-three, I will give you a real make-up demonstration!"

She told me she had never seen those girls work so well or so cheerfully. They finished everything asked of them on time. You see they had a purpose to work for.

(b) *This is needed for later*

Thinking ahead will always help us to complete tasks

which we don't fancy. The burning desire held in mind will make us finish the less desirable task in order to do the things we enjoy doing.

Ambition is a useful spur to the persons studying, especially when they imagine themselves passing the examinations. The very thought of success injects energy into the effort.

(c) *Make a game of it*

This often works wonders, and not only for children. Our imagination will assist our concentration in completing the job on hand.

I have seen a group of sixteen people tackle a long tedious job of checking through all the books in a small school library.

The person organising the check made it "a military operation" with the promise of a "Victory" supper when the enemy was defeated. Amid all the work, jokes and humour played a vital role until the task was completed.

Complete concentration was needed during this so-called miserable job. But because of the challenge and the game of "soldiers" all was done—happily and correctly.

(d) *Take the task as a challenge*

There are times when we ought to concentrate on something that is just immeasurably dull. All of us have experienced this at sometime in our lives.

It pays to ask yourself if this work on hand is going to defeat me. Then treat this work as an enemy and go out and lick it. When you have completed the task you feel successful and happy.

2 *Make an effort.*

Some techniques as I have mentioned are useful in making an effort to concentrate: But another point should be made. Concentration is not always easy to achieve, and one of the most important aspects of the art of concentrating is that we must train ourselves to *recall* our attention.

Of course attention wanders. Unless the subject is of overwhelming personal interest, no-one's mind can stay on it for long. 20 minutes of uninterrupted concentration is quite good. The fatal (and extremely common) mistake is to give up as soon as the first concentration begins to weaken.

The effort should come then. Jerk yourself back to the task in hand every five minutes.

It should be understood clearly that the person who last week could not concentrate on his/her work for more than five minutes at a time, and who this week can persist for ten minutes without having to force the thoughts back to the subject in hand, has in fact achieved an enormous victory.

Such progress points the way to further progress, until we can continue to concentrate for longer periods. All skills are acquired gradually—with many lapses on the way to success.

I believe we must put ourselves under some pressure to achieve good results. A goal setting plan acts as a stimulus and we can look back on a satisfactory effort.

3. *Remove distractions*

If I were asked to give one single hint for efficient study to a school child or student—it would be "Never switch the radio or television on during a study period." I am convinced that the habit of having a radio programme on in the background is bad for concentration. I know I trained myself to study and write with music blaring away—but it took time and effort to achieve this. But concentration has to be learned, and first of all we should aim at cutting down the distractions.

So the key is to finish the work programme first of all and then to relax and listen to the radio or watch television.

4. *Relax*

Relaxation is a skill, like concentration it has to be learned. If we allow our muscles to become tense, we cannot do well. The essential relationship between relaxation and concentration is this: We waste energy everytime we allow ourselves to be tense. Tension feels uncomfortable and discomfort is a distraction; and tension impairs actual efficiency.

Under all circumstances staleness or over fatigue must be avoided. Once you are in such a condition you will never be able to concentrate or achieve very much. This danger can be avoided by ordered times of study interspersed with adequate change and recreation.

5. *Concentration helps you to get things done*

Maybe the following ideas will help you to concentrate and give you a better understanding of how to make your life somewhat easier.

(a) *Plan your programme.* A planned programme helps us to concentrate on the task in hand. Otherwise we are inclined to flit from one thing to another. A daily diary is a useful aid to this.

(b) *Know what you want.* When you know what you want, it becomes easier to adapt to the project at hand.

Concentration is now your friend and not the enemy. When you get excited over what you are aiming for your mind is on the goal.

(c) *Life is a game.* Now play it with intense effort and enjoy the challenges. Victory is yours when you play to win.

(d) *Read stories of successful people.* There are many books written about people who failed and yet conquered the glory of life. Read them and you will find your concentration will improve as you become absorbed in the contents.

FINALLY

Concentration is never easy. It requires effort and more effort to overcome outside interferences. But we have to persevere until we are truly successful.

In our quest for concentration we are, in reality, fighting the infant that lives on in all of us. We are seeking, to become more adult, more mature.

In acquiring greater powers of concentration, we are doing more than enabling ourselves to work more efficiently. We are improving the qualities of our most priceless possession—the human mind.

9 *How to conquer an inferiority complex*

Inferiority feeling is like a prison from which there seems to be no deliverance. And yet the chains are not welded by others but by the individuals themselves.

"People have only to look at me to begin to humiliate and ridicule" a Cape woman wrote to me recently. What she did not realise was that her subconscious mannerism and gestures were an invitation to others to take advantage of her advertised inferiority.

If your subconscious mind takes pains to appear to others in the guise of a worm, you must expect them to tread on you.

The expressions of inferiority feeling are varied. "People come to resent and hate me" said one woman. A man complained that in the presence of other people he feels a nobody.

Others find that they appear clumsy in the company of strangers or even friends.

Many know that all these inferiority feelings have their origin in the earliest years of life. A psychologist friend of mine said "so many people felt rejected in their childhood that is why they feel unwanted as adults". He went on to say "the thing is to realise it and be rejected no longer."

I wish it were really as simple as that. But it is not. What he said is true, as far as it goes, but it doesn't go far enough.

However much you crave to overcome your deep inferiority, you will never do so unless you understand yourself on an unusually deep level—the level of your emotional habits. Only then can you recognise the emotional system you have worked out unwittingly for yourself.

Your first task is to see where your problem is rooted in personal history. It is true to say, I believe that the problem of inferiority is the problem of rejection.

Children are born to parents who do not love them. Or they cannot give the baby the kind of acceptance and love that meets its need.

Some mothers have a dislike for breast feeding. Some have to help to maintain the family and so must go to work. Some are temperamentally unsuited to be mothers. Some are unwilling to try.

Some spoil their children with gifts but starve them of care and affection. Some are too particular about marks on the furniture.

Sense of Guilt

From whatever cause, the baby feels that he or she does not belong. It is a matter of urgency for the child to have union with his mother. But every time they feel frustrated.

The child fears for his or her survival. Feeling guilty and punishable for unknown crimes.

The reason for this is obvious when we think about it. While the baby gets no rapport, sympathy or union with the mother, and feels angry about this, he finds himself unable to accuse the mother because he is completely at her mercy.

Indeed, to save himself (herself) from his anger toward the mother, he comes to the point where he turns all his anger against himself. He is ready to punish himself for crimes he, of course never committed.

That is why lots of children have a permanent sense of guilt toward their parents.

Sometimes when parents quarrel between themselves in the hearing of their baby, the baby becomes terrified. He may even take all the blames upon himself.

As a result, he no longer looks for a life of love and fulfilment, nor believe it is possible. Hope, prospects, fulfilments are out, and he learns an emotional reaction of hopelessness. This becomes his life.

He feels deeply rejected and a total loss. This scars his personality so deeply, he cannot believe in the possibility of things being different.

"You can't make a silk purse out of a sow's ear" said one sufferer to me. Deeper than any other conviction was that he was "different" he was certain that a real change was impossible. To him, his position was that of a nobody.

This is the predicament of the "inferior" person. You feel yourself to be a reject.

The inferior person feels that he has everything but the essential ingredients that would give him "authority."

Here then is the background of inferiority feelings.

If a baby accepts the fact of his no goodness, rejection, hopelessness and difference, what can he do?

If he is to survive at all he must take measures in order to cope as best as he can. Man's strongest urge is for survival and the measures the infant takes have one end in view, to save him from the intolerable void of futility and non-significance.

To obviate this supreme catastrophe various methods are chosen by the infant.

One for instance, will put on an act and pretend to be something he isn't. In later years he develops into the person who compensates for inferiority by a sham superiority. Some become cynical and a know-all.

If he is a cold intellectual, he will overcome you or try to—with his "wisdom" and "knowledge".

If the parental forces have been completely overwhelming in young years, the adult tends to develop a role of defeatism.

Yet others take the role of being pushed around and persecuted. They expect everything to go wrong. Naturally if that is what they expect—their expectations are fulfilled.

Is there a way to be rid of this terrible inferiority feeling? I have known many people accomplish this victory, but it is not lightly achieved. It depends on determination and on constant effort. But it *can* be done if you can take the challenge seriously enough.

Here is a programme of self-help. If faithfully carried out in a practical way, it will achieve your objective and help you for the first time in life to become a real person. I suggest three stages.

1. *Look deeply at your foundation*

Study the first part of this article several times. It will help you to lay hold on the crux of the problem, which is that the present non-esteem is built on a lie.

That lie needs to be replaced by the truth. And the truth must be firmly established in the deepest recesses of the personality where the lie has been recorded.

When the walls of Winchester Cathedral began to crack, it was found that the ancient foundations were a set of wooden logs, rotting because they were resting on a bog. Engineers took out the logs one by one and replaced each one with pressurised concrete. This saved the cathedral.

Your hope lies in a similar process. You are now realising that the nonentity you feel yourself to be is far from being the whole truth. Indeed, it is not true at all, even though your present personality or lack of it has been founded on this lie.

You need, therefore, to replace the foundations of hopelessness, rejection and nonentity with the concrete realities of wholeness, value and acceptance.

But this awareness of wholeness, value and acceptance must get deep enough to provide for you the permanent foundation for your new life.

You must clearly see that your sense of unacceptability and hopelessness comes from earlier days and was imposed upon you by an unfortunate history. These unfortunate foundations have to be replaced by the firm reality that you are a child of God.

You need to thrill to the fact that given the right course of action and thought, your true personality can unfold to the perfection it potentially is.

2. *Learn the art of recognising your unconscious responses*

Progress from inferiority to a glowing sense of acceptance will in part depend upon your ability to recognise that most of your bad feelings about yourself and those around you come from inward negative thoughts.

It is a matter of catching yourself out in your moods so that at anytime you can see through them to what lies beneath—your repudiation of yourself as a worthwhile person.

You need to be able to recognise too, that these moods of hopelessness, guilt and inadequency (or maybe the show of pattern of superiority, aggressiveness or defeatism) are the

62

emotional foods on which you have lived through many a long year.

You need to replace this diet of unhappiness with the joys of acceptance and love.

This is I know is not easy—but needs to be repeated every day. You are exchanging one set of thoughts for another. Only then will you see how wonderful you really are.

3. *Use a self-conditioning formula*

Self-conditioning will help inject your new ideas into your subconscious mind. You might construct a self-conditioning formula on these lines:

Whenever my fundamental energies express themselves in worthlessness and the hopelessness of inferiority. That is the signal for me instead to invest these same energies in a warm acceptance of myself as good and in a positive appreciation of my very own personality.

This formula or any other which will change the morbid for a new dynamic approach to life—must be repeated daily until it becomes part of you. The real you.

If correctly used it brings some immediate results.

Take courage. If you are in earnest, a new life will open for you.

10 *How to win through in spite of setbacks in your life*

Few of us escape disappointments and setbacks of one kind or another. Some people seem to get more than their share, but no one is immune.

A young man fails in an important examination, or just misses some coveted prize, another is passed over for some keenly awaited promotion. Illness intervenes—causing financial difficulties in a family. Or a young girl's romance falls apart on the eve of marriage.

These are things that happen every day. Reactions vary. Some victims hide their feelings. This is the exception rather than the rule.

All too often the reaction to these experiences is vexation, resentment and bitterness. Some simply freeze and refuse to talk about it. Others can think or talk about nothing else.

In either case this thing that has happened to them has become an obsession. It fills their whole way of thinking. It leaves them nothing but unhappy thoughts, which can breed a cynical attitude to everybody and everything.

What is one to do? How can we avert such a tragedy in our own life? How can we avoid misfortune (if it should come) spoiling us for really happy and worthwhile living?

First and foremost I suggest that, up against some setback and disappointment, you try to preserve a sense of proportion. What hits us personally is apt to make it look bigger than it really is.

Suppose, then, this hard-knock or setback happened to somebody else. Would it seem so serious? The probability is, it would not. Looking at it in a detached and unemotional way, you might even think it trifling.

THE LONG VIEW

Secondly, we should cultivate the Long View. Things are not always what they seem at the time. Life goes on and the sequel may disprove and dispel what worried and disappointed us so much at the time.

The road of life, it has been truly said, is more like a lane than a road. Its horizons are very limited. We can't see far ahead. You never can tell what the future will be or how things will eventually turn out.

The unhappy experience of yesterday may turn out to be blessings in disguise in some future tomorrow.

A girl's broken romance may turn out to be the best thing that could have happened to her, as many a happily married woman in later years has discovered and would be the first to admit.

The job we don't get and the important positions we are not asked to fill are not always the calamities they seem. You may find that they wouldn't have given you the scope for your powers which your present position does give.

Such happy surprises don't always occur. But keep the possibility in mind. Cultivate the long view and trust the future. You never can tell.

A healthy courageous reaction to the setbacks and disappointments we meet can produce positive results of the highest value.

Let us take the case of Sir Walter Scott. In his middle years he was bankrupt. He resolved his problems by his writings to pay off all his debts—which at that time was a vast amount.

Before this he had only written poetry. Now he switched to historical romance. Through challenging and battling years, he paid off all his debts, writing master pieces which gave him a fame far beyond anything he had known before.

Would Scott have achieved his greatness but for his adversity? I doubt it. The necessity that he had to face made him find his potential—which otherwise would have been dormant.

The same idea is expressed in the saying "Necessity is the mother of invention." Extremity calls out fresh resources of mind and skill to match the need. What are we to learn from this?

Setbacks and hindrances can be used to fashion future success. Not only so they may be the spur and incentive we need but to reveal our full powers and capacities.

The all-determining factor is you—your attitude of mind and spirit. If you are a defeatist, and just prepared to regard the whole business as hopeless, nothing will come out of it.

Switch your mind and attitude to things in the opposite direction, to the positives.

Face your situation realistically. Instead of moaning about your hard luck, be humble enough to ask yourself "may not the blame be partly, at least mine?"

The star golfer, for instance, doesn't reach the top merely by constant and presistent practice, but by intelligent practice. From time to time he discovers mistakes, masters them, and thereby acquires what is for him the perfect technique for victory.

Learn from your setbacks and disappointments.

Lord Reith, the founder of the British Broadcasting Corporation, in his autobiography says: "I don't ask for difficulties, but when they come I welcome them as a challenge." Later he adds: "I feel happiest when I am fully stretched".

Accepting, then, your hardship as a challenge, go forward with confidence and courage and faith, that you have what it takes. You are not at the limit of your powers and potentialities. There is more there waiting to be used.

Says Karl Menninger, the noted psychiatrist "Think big, believe big and act big". To this add work and struggle. This is the formula for gaining the victory over defeats. The full strength potential within you becomes mobilised to see you through".

What is failing in an examination or some business venture compared to tragic happenings like losing someone dear to you, or becoming permanently incapacitated by losing a limb, or becoming blind or maybe totally deaf?

Of course there is no comparison. And yet the all-important thing is your mental and emotional attitude. Someone said to a young professional man, who was growing blind, "How this must colour your whole view of things!" He bravely replied "But it's for me to choose the colour!"

I suggest the following steps

Acceptance of what has happened is the first step to overcoming the consequence of any misfortune. It only aggravates the trouble by getting all worked up and angrily muttering "Why should this happen to me"? Whatever the hurt or adversity, try to accept it for what it is without bitterness, resentment or self-pity. Face up to the fact that somehow or other you must adjust yourself to it.

I like the simple prayer:

"God grant me the serenity to accept the things I cannot change; the courage to change the things I can, and the wisdom to know the difference".

It is sometimes amazing what can be achieved in spite of the worst disabilities, where there is a mind and a determination to exploit every possibility. Think of Douglas Bader the legless airman who learned to walk almost normally with artificial limbs, and became a wartime fighter pilot.

There is always something left. It is for you to cooperate with that.

Sir William Robertson Nicoll, one of the great newspaper editors in the early years of the century, was a gifted young minister in a Scottish village. Then his vocal chords became paralysed.

He was never able to speak above a whisper for the rest of his life. At the same time, his wife died, leaving several children to care for.

He turned courageously to freelance journalism, and eventually established himself as one of the most influential journalists in England. He founded "British Weekly" and many other journals which finally brought him fame and a knighthood.　　William Nicoll had learned the secret of cooperating with the inevitable and utilising to the utmost limit what he had.　　A noted psychologist once said that "When we stop fighting the inevitable, we release energy, which enables us to create a richer life".

To maintain courage up against odds and adversities in life, we need a resurgence of faith—faith in God and ourselves in the knowledge that eventually we win through.

It was said "Pray your way through your problems and difficulties".

Alexis Carrell a famous psychologist—gave these scientific facts. "Prayer is the most powerful form of energy one can generate, prayer like radium is a source of self-generating energy. When we pray, we link ourselves with the power of the universe; our human deficiencies are filled and we arise strengthened and prepared."

Have faith to believe—then go into action. Leave behind the doubts and fears. I have broadcast many times do not belong to the P.L.O.M. Club. "The poor little old me club". This gets you nowhere. But helps you to become unwell in mind and body.

The following thoughts were said many years ago.

"No longer forward nor behind I look in hope and fear; but grateful take the good I find the best of now and here."

"Life is worth living—that is the point to remember, life is well worth what it costs. It is short and we must make the most of it."

Always expect the best—express the best and finally the best will come to you.

11 *Getting rid of your feeling of depression*

TODAY IN SOUTH AFRICA THERE SEEMS TO BE MORE UNHAPPY DEPRESSED PEOPLE THAN EVER BEFORE: WHAT CAN WE DO ABOUT IT?

Whatever feelings we have, including depression, we can be sure that they are shared by other people. We are not alone in our troubles.

It is because we do not know all the other people personally that we develop the false idea that what is happening to us is unique. Because it seems special to us we come to think that we are different from other people.

With the thousands of letters I receive via the radio programmes, I can assure you that there are many who are in the same situation: what with retrenchment, pay cuts, high interest and mortgage rates—increase in food prices and many other such problems.

Our feelings, including depression, therefore become more and more important to us and more and more of a worry.

The conviction that we are not alone in our misery, that others feel the same, makes the depression less important and so less frightening.

First of all we need to be sure about our health because if we are unwell it is not surprising that we become depressed. Even anxiety about health, wondering what is wrong and whether it is something serious, makes us depressed. So have a physical check up. This can be done at the local hospital. The cost is small so don't delay.

There are other obvious causes like the shock of a sudden bereavement, and the pressure of coping with this. A couple were both retrenched from their jobs on the same day. These challenges can undermine our self-confidence and bring on a feeling of rejection. It even affects our security—our feeling of being needed?

Whatever form our difficulties take, we have to remind ourselves that what has happened has happened. Do not permit yourself to nurse grief, disappointment, bitterness, despair, beyond a reasonable period. Be most concerned with the present life—as it is now.

Fits of depression waste time and effort as we remain brooding over what-might-have-been if only everything had stayed the same.

An example is that of a woman who came to consult me about her depression. Each member of her family had left South Africa to settle in different parts of the world. Her husband had died several years ago, now she was alone. What am I to do, how can I cope alone? Being a reasonably wealthy woman she could travel and visit each of her children from time to time. I told her she could now be excited as the opportunity to travel was a new adventure. Instead of loneliness new doors were opening.

I pointed out she was far more fortunate than most who did not have money to do what she was now able to do.

We have to look outwards towards other people and the outside world instead of just thinking about ourselves.

Fresh opportunities will surely come, always assuming that we are prepared to look for them.

Become interested in other people, find fulfilment in
service to others, and slowly but surely we find happiness
as well.

Conversely, when we allow depression to become a habit
we get bogged down with self-pity.

If you want to get rid of depression, you must remain in
charge of your thoughts. Although your doctor can help,
and your family and friends give you support, in the long
run it is up to you.

Nobody can make you feel better if you, yourself, are not
prepared to co-operate. You have to keep on trying, even
when you do not feel like it, even when it seems no use.

I shall never forget how one of the grandest characters in
radio when asked what was the secret of his constant
cheerfulness—replied: "When I wake up in the morning, I
say to myself 'Now, my boy, which is it going to be today?
Are you going to be happy, or are you going to be
miserable?' And I just decide to be happy."

There is a little over-simplification in this recipe for
cheerfulness but, in it, there is a tremendous truth. We
need to train our feelings diligently to express themselves in
a fulfilling and happy way, and to encourage happiness to
come from our efforts.

Many of us who were brought up in the U.K. during the
great depression of the early 1930's know what problems
are. Lack of money—few if any jobs and little prospects of
anything better. But through effort, faith and trust it all
came to pass. Bringing with it a new feeling: "We did it."

Let me tell you the story of Edward Bok a Hollander who
came to America with his family.

"I was born of well-to-do parents but when I was six

years old my father lost all his wealth, and faced life at forty-five, in a strange country, without even necessities.

"I had the handicap of not knowing one word of the English language. I went to a public school and learned what I could. The boys were cruel, as boys are. The teachers were impatient, as tired teachers are. There was no money.

"So, after school hours, my brother and I went home, but not to play—but to help a mother who daily grew more frail. Not for days, but for years, we two boys got up in the gray cold winter dawn to sift the coal ashes to find unburned coal. Then we set the table for the scant breakfast—went to school—came home and washed the dishes and even scrubbed the floors.

"At ten years of age I got my first job—washing windows in a baker's shop at fifty cents a week. Then I began to sell the bread to earn more money. Saturday mornings I delivered newspapers. Later on, I became a reporter during the evenings—an office boy during the day.

"There is not a single step on the road of direct poverty that I do not know of or have not experienced. And having experienced every thought, every feeling and every hardship that comes to those who travel that road, I say today: That I rejoice with everyone who is going through the same experience.

"I believe in poverty as a condition to experience, to go through and then to get out of: not as a condition to stay in. No two persons can find the same way out. Each must find his way for himself. I was determined to get out of poverty—that thought was the essential for my success—for now I had a purpose."

Finally Edward Bok became one of the greatest journalists in America and eventually owned several magazines.

I have told this story to show that even in South Africa at the present time when things appear tough—through will power—faith and belief we will come through this challenge and be better people for having experienced the doubts and fears.

A bankrupt businessman came to see me with his wife one evening. His opening words were "I am ruined, everything we have has gone". After a moment of silence and before I could say something the wife said to her husband—"will you and me and the children be sold up" "of course not" he replied. Then don't say we have lost everything. All that is most valuable still remains: "Our love for each other. Possessions may have gone—but we can make another fortune if our hearts and hands are used with fortitude and courage. The dear wife had given a much greater answer than I could have done.

We must rehearse to ourselves the glorious fact that the problems—difficulties—grief and loss we are now facing will pass.

There is a right way for every emergency and if we give ourselves the dignity and importance that is ours by right—we shall soon go forward to conquer.

You are of measureless worth. You have infinite capacity. You have powers within you which, disciplined, can bring you to goals you thought were impossible before.

As you recognize your potential and the talents you were given you can only go forward.

You must now know your importance. You must build up your own knowledge of yourself. You must exercise your decisiveness, your compassion and love.

Getting rid of your feeling of depression

NEVER FEEL BEATEN

We can make the mistake of basing our happiness and assessing our success solely on income and the things we can afford to buy.

Not to keep up with friends and neighbours. To have to make do with the same car. To many this is a sign of failure.

How easy it is to lose sight of what really matters when our sense of values goes wrong?

The best way never to feel beaten is to envy no one. Success without health is a poor thing. Money without love is mockery.

Get your goals right: Don't be put off—wait for the right time to move. Reserve your energy for the essentials.

Follow these ideas and you need never be beaten.

12 *Personality as a success asset*

PART ONE

Your personality is the sum total of your characteristics and appearances which distinguish you from all others. The clothes you wear, the lines in your face, the tone of your voice, the thoughts you think, the character you have developed by those thoughts, all constitute parts of your personality.

The charm of personality is a gift that can sway the strongest of characters. Those who possess the rare quality of a pleasing personality influence all those about them.

The charming personality of women more often or not is a trait that far excels personal beauty. What could be more desirable than a personality which always attracts, never repels? It is not only valuable to women, but to all in every field of life. No matter what career you enter, you cannot overestimate the importance of cultivating the personal qualities which attract people to you. The whole principle of a pleasing personality lies in one sentence: A positive personality attracts: a negative personality repels.

There are many attributes that make up a strong and vibrant personality.

In this two part series I am listing and describing those assets which reveal a positive personality:

(1) Character.
(2) Courage.
(3) Courtesy.

 (4) Decision making.
 (5) Emotional control.
 (6) Enthusiasm.
 (7) Honesty.
 (8) Kindness.
 (9) Love.
(10) Loyalty.
(11) Patience.
(12) Personal appearance.
(13) Punctuality.
(14) Sincerity.
(15) Tolerance.

You will find there are many more you can add but I have tried to convey those which to me are extremely important.

(1) *Character*

Character is power, character is influence and with only this a person is eminently useful, not only to family and friend—but to society and to God.

There is a difference between character and reputation. Character is what a person is; reputation is what he or she is thought to be. Character comes from within; reputation is without. Character is a person's real worth. Reputation is their market place. A man or woman may have a good character and a bad reputation; or a good reputation but a poor character. We form our opinions of what people appear to be.

Character is something you cannot buy. You get it only by building it; and you can build it by your own thoughts and deeds.

"Through the aid of auto-suggestion, any person can acquire a sound character, no matter what his past has been.

How strange that a young woman will stand many hours a day, for years, practicing on a piano or training her voice; that a young man will give years of hard and long study to the mastering of a profession or occupation; and yet be unwilling to spend any considerable time in building a character that will insure absolute peace of mind, contentment and happiness under all circumstances.

It was once written: "Remember that your real worth can be measured, not by what you have, but by what you are".

Strength of character consists of two things—power of will and power of self-control. It requires two things, for its existence—strong feelings and command over them.

(2) *Courage*

Courage is not the absence of fear, it is the conquest of it.

Peter Marshall said—"God, gives us the courage to stand for something lest we fall for anything."

The greater part of the courage that is needed in the world is not of an heroic kind. We need the common courage to be honest, to resist temptation, to speak the truth, the courage to be true to ourselves and not pretend to be what we are not. We must have the courage to think our own thoughts and speak our own feelings and form our own convictions.

A proverb of India says of courage "Hope and courage are two bright diamonds in the crown of success".

May you possess this crown!

(3) *Courtesy*

An old proverb reads:

"If we could all be courteous for even a single day, the hatreds of humanity would turn to love".

What a joy it would be if we could all try this method of living. Courtesy and politeness are one and the same thing. In this hustling and bustling world in which we live courtesy seems to have been pushed into the background. In many a home politeness is not taught. This must not be left to school teachers. It is the responsibility of parents. If parents were not careless about the manners of their children at home they would not be shocked at what they hear about them from other people.

True politeness is always to have regards for the comforts of others. It has been said many times "That manners maketh the man".

A young man was being interviewed for a certain job. When the manager walked into the room the young man did not get up, also he was smoking a cigarette. Needless to say he did not get the job. The manager first of all was put off by the casualness and secondly he could not stand the smell of a cigarette.

When I give talks to school girls and boys, I try and impress upon them, that courtesy pays dividends. Respect for others opens many doors and most people respond positively to politeness.

Daily experience has taught me that civility is not only one of the essentials of success but the impression it creates is so rewarding.

Take time to study yourself and make sure that one of your attributes is good manners. As I said at the begin-

ning—it starts in the home and by the parents example
will children follow.

(4) *Decision makings*

This is one of the most challenging problems. How many
of us fail to commit ourselves to making a firm decision and
working to see it become a successful one. Most people are
procrastinators waiting for something to happen, and of
course nothing does without action. The poem procrastination tells the story.

I'll do it all tomorrow
for tomorrow never comes.
I promise you for sure I'll do it then.
I shall positively feel
a tremendous lot of zeal—
be a whirl of dynamism once again.

I'll do it all tomorrow
that I promise faithfully.
I'll rise all bright and eager in the dawn;
I'll astonish all the neighbours
with my energetic labours,
and I'll be the go-est getter ever born.

I'll do it all tomorrow
when I've planned the thing with care.
I'll get down and buckle to it, come what may.
What I really can't allow
is to do it here and now;
for I've planned a lot of nothing for today.

I have learnt by experience that one can work oneself
into the mood appropriate for the task on hand.

The decisive person is the one who copes with life's problems and deals with them with vigour and effort.

(5) *Emotional Control*

To often self-control is made to mean only the control of angry passions, but that is simply one form of self-control: it means the control over all passions, appetites, and impulses.

It is necessary to one's personal happiness to exercise control over his words as well as his acts, for there are words that strike even harder than blows.

In my counselling with couples who are talking about separation or divorce I find it is the lack of emotional control that causes so much misery. Recently I saw a married couple who for the past eight years have done nothing else but bicker. No way have they been able to sit down and iron out the problems. During their period with me they continued to pick each other out, until I stopped them and asked "What do you want". Their failure to communicate and discuss day to day challenges that all married persons have to deal with was really the cause. To be able to control the emotions when it seems easier to fly into a temper is hard—but must be worked at until you can really say we are two matured people. When you are desperate and unable to control yourself—always ask "What do I want". If it is to stay married then find a solution to the problem. If it is a business problem ask again "What do I want". Then seek a solution. Lack of emotional control solves nothing—but brings hurts and unhappiness.

(6) *Enthusiasm*

Enthusiasm is faith in action. Nearly all of the great improvements, discoveries, inventions, and achievements have started with the person involved having had enthusiasm.

Enthusiasm comes from the Greek "En Theos" which means the "God within".

There is, perhaps, no mistake of a young man more common than that of supposing that, in the pursuits of life, extraordinary talents are necessary to achieve success. Enthusiasm, with a moderate degree of wisdom, will carry a person farther than any amount of intellect without it. It gives the person force and momentum.

The people who have most powerfully influenced the world have not been so much persons of genius but being strong in convictions in their capacity of work impelled by enthusiasm and determination.

I am hoping the youth of today will not lose their enthusiasm for living. As they bubble with excitement and hope they will pave the way for a better life for all.

It was written in a business journal—if a man can maintain enthusiasm long enough, it will produce anything.

How then can you acquire this blessed gift of enthusiasm? Some people seem to be born with it. But to those who claim they have not got it (and there are plenty around today) they can change. They have to learn to ignite the fire which at times is nearly out.

First you must believe in yourself, in your own value, in your abilities to do what you want to do. Don't let others talk you down.

You must give yourself whole-heartedly to anything you set your hand to. Then treat each day as a new adventure and be happy in what you do.

Your thoughts filled with enthusiasm can change a second-rate thinker to a first-rate achiever.

Join the ranks of the enthusiasts. Life for you will grow richer and more worthwhile.

Enthusiasm will open a door when other ways fail

13 *Personality as a success asset*

PART TWO

In the previous chapter I gave my thoughts on how to develop a successful personality and concluding the article on enthusiasm, having mentioned—character—courage—courtesy—decision making—emotional control.

Now to continue with the next ideas to give one a successful personality.

(7) *Honesty*

I wonder how many of us are honest with ourselves. Many believe that honesty relates primarily to business transactions, but to be honest with ourselves is the starting point to happiness. It means that you must understand your strengths and weaknesses. Shakespeare wrote: "To thine own self be true, for as surely as night will follow day, thou cans't not be false to any man."

Honesty and trust go hand in hand. When we as parents trust each other we develop an honest approach to all we do. There are then no questions asked of each others activities—other than an honest interest. Then children relate to parents and early on in their lives they become totally honest with the parents. Parents tell the children we "trust you." They in turn have then no reasons to lie about anything they have done. It is sad when children feel they must lie in order to avoid some punishment, instead of being taught to stand up and admit a mistake. This attitude often determines their future. Yes honesty plays such an important role in our lives.

(8) *Kindness*

Ralph Wardo Emerson said:

"You cannot do a kindness too soon, for you never know how soon it will be too late."

Kindness makes sunshine wherever it goes. When we are kind to each other the best of a person is shown. Little kindnesses are great ones. They help to drive away sadness and bring a cheer in the lives of many. Who can rightly estimate the ultimate effect of one kind word spoken to someone who feels down and unwanted.

Speak kindly in the morning; it lightens all the cares of the day and makes the household and other affairs move along more smoothly. Speak kindly at night; for to some members of a family it forms contentment. Speak kindly at all times; it encourages many and can awaken a person to greater achievement. Always leave home with kind words and leave behind a feeling of goodwill.

(9) *Love*

An Indian proverb says, "If there be love, impossibilities will become possible" love is the ruling element of life.

Genuine love is founded on esteem and respect. I believe there is no greater love than a mother for a child. No matter what the child may have done, been rude—stolen money or even has killed someone, the mother is always ready to forgive.

The following thoughts were written—author unknown: "Mend a quarrel. Search out a forgotten friend. Dismiss suspicion and replace it with trust. Write a love letter. Share some treasure. Give a soft answer. Encourage youth. Manifest your loyalty in a word or deed. Keep a promise.

Find the time. Forego a grudge. Forgive an enemy. Listen. Apologize if you were wrong. Try to understand. Flout envy. Examine your demands on others. Think first of someone else. Appreciate, be kind, be gentle. Laugh a little more. Deserve confidence. Take up arms against malice. Decry complacency. Express your gratitude. Worship your God. Gladden the heart of a child. Take pleasure in the beauty and wonder of the earth. Speak your love. Speak it again. Speak it still again. Speak it still once more."

If we could all live by these ideals what a joy life would be. What a great world it would become. For truly love does find a way.

"Love life and live love"

---

(10) *Loyalty*

Loyalty is the faithful, constant exercise, of and devotion to a duty or obligation owing to someone or something. Faithfulness, constancy, and loyalty are similar in nature, but different in degrees. Faithfulness implies a steadfast fidelity to an obligation or duty. Constancy suggests firmness and steadfastness in attachment. Loyalty implies unswerving allegiance to something or someone.

Our first loyalty should be to God and mankind. This is borne out in the words of Jesus when he said "Thou shalt love the Lord thy God with all thy heart, and with all thy soul and with all thy mind. This is the first and great commandment. And the second is like unto it, thou shalt love thy neighbour as thyself. On these two commandments hang all the law and the prophets."

To be loyal is to be true to your womanhood or manhood. Be loyal and true to your obligations so long as you are under such an obligation. This applies to marriage —business or what profession we find ourselves in. Loyalty in marriage is a sacred commitment and one we must not take too lightly. It is the offspring of loving and caring.

I spell loyalty, using the word care!

C. Commitment.
A. Attitude.
R. Responsibility.
E. Enthusiasm.

Success is built upon loyalty, faith, sincerity, cooperation and other positive forces.

(11) *Patience*

How much of home happiness and comfort depends upon the exercise of patience! Not a day passes when patience is needed in family life. Let the parents learn to be patient with their children. They still have much to learn and when you are very young you require everything you want straight away. Care and time will soon enough check their childish impulses. Children should be taught at an early age the need of patience, of how to cure a bad temper. But it depends on the adults in the home to set the right example.

In these times of everything that must be instant it is difficult to quiet the mind and learn to relax.

Watch how we shop at the supermarket and how irritable everyone is. I believe impatience is the cause of many ailments. We burn ourselves out—when we rush around in a state of nerves.

Let us try to ease life's burdens, with a little more tolerance and kindness towards all persons we meet. It's worth trying if we wish to be healthy and happy.

(12) *Personal Appearance*

It is good to know that we are our own best advertisements. Whatever one's business it is worthwhile to dress accordingly.

Neatness of dress, cleanliness and the manner of the applicant are the first things an employer notices in a would be employee.

You may say an employer ought to be a reader of real merit, real character, and that it is not fair to estimate an applicant for a position by such superficial things as the clothes he wears. But unfortunately we are so often judged by the first appearance of contact.

Sometime ago a young man came to see me because he couldn't find a job. He had a B.A. degree, a first class matric and was extremely bright. But he cared little about his appearance—very long hair—always went for an interview in jeans. I pointed out the need was for him to obtain a position. So conform—get a haircut, look presentable and start again. In one week he was fixed up. It goes to show that we are our own best advertisements.

(13) *Punctuality*

One of the great virtues is where possible to be on time. This is so important that I wonder why it is not taught at home, in schools and business.

I note at times how casual we become when we go to work. Five or ten minutes late seems to be a pattern many have acquired. Yet success and happiness depend in a far higher degree on punctuality than many suppose. It is not sufficient to do the right thing, but it must be done at the right time as well.

The punctual person has the advantage of being relaxed and at ease. They save energy because they have not put themselves under pressure due to leaving things too late.

Many times we note that an unpunctual person is not trusted with a particular task as the employer feels that he or she is not responsible.

Most great leaders in commerce, industry and in professions are good examples to follow. They are keen on the ball and first at work.

(14) *Sincerity*

Sincerity is one of the most important traits of a pleasing personality that a person can have in the pursuit of happiness or success. Sincerity means honesty and truthfulness from the heart and the complete absence of deceitfulness. Deceit and falsehood are obstacles to happiness.

To find a person who cares about others and goes out of his or her way to help someone—without any form of payment of any kind.

We can take a lesson from children for they are the personification of sincerity. It is true that being such, they often cause embarrassment, but it is well to note that it isn't the sincerity that causes the embarrassment, but the expression of it. One trait doesn't make a character or a pleasing personality. It is the combination of ingredients necessary. So, too, in the expression of our sincerity we need to exercise tact and self-discipline.

Henry David Thoreau wrote: "Man's noblest gift to man is his sincerity, for it embraces his integrity also."

(15) *Tolerance*

Tolerance stands high on the list of the traits of a winning and pleasing personality. Without tolerance regardless of the number of other traits a person possesses, he could not possibly have a magnetic personality.

An intolerant person is one who is unable to tolerate contrary opinions. Carrying this a step further, this means that an intolerant person does not recognize the right of another individual to have an opinion of his own if it is the opposite of his own ideas.

Today in South Africa tolerance is really needed so that we can learn to understand each others points of view.

Tolerance does not mean we have agreed with everyone or every statement made. But it does mean we might not agree with someone, but respect that they have an opinion of there own.

So in closing this chapter let us pride ourselves that we do have great personalities. Some of us may have to do a little homework to correct a few mistakes. But we have all got one. Let's use it to the full.

14 *A ten point plan for succeeding in your career*

Anyone who wishes to succeed in his or her career can generally do so by merit—hard work, loyalty and persistence.

It is true that even in the best of worlds, people may occasionally suffer set backs through things outside of their control. But it is much more a certainty and generally true that most unsuccessful people are their own victims.

How then can success be achieved?

Usually it is achieved by a mixture of effort and planning. The following ten points can assist in a person's future.

1. *Learn your job*

As soon as you enter a new job, go out of your way to learn everything possible about it. What is the daily routine? How do things work? What is the quickest method of doing something? What is expected of you? Develop a questioning mind. The sooner you master the daily routines the quicker you adapt to your new position.

I went into a newspaper office to place an advertisement. The young lady who attended to me had only started that day. She said I am sorry if I appear slow but am finding my way in this new job. Her right attitude, smile and asking help from a senior. Soon had everything under control. As it was her first day, she had certainly learned a lot already.

A person who intends to make a real career should never

stop studying. At all times we have to keep up-to-date with new developments.

2. *Do your job*

This statement may sound strange—but how many persons do you know—who barely do their job—efficiently—happily and give of their best at all times. So many employees arrive late for work, chat around the office or factory, spend longer times than necessary over tea or coffee. If we steal time we are in fact being dishonest. I believe we have to give good service in whatever direction we have chosen, not just to satisfy the superior, but to have the satisfaction of knowing we have done our level best.

3. *Then do a little more*

Remember I am referring to a person who wants to make a successful career of his or her life.

Someone who is prepared to do more than they are paid to do. Not just a clock watcher, but a dynamic doer.

A middle-aged woman needed a job badly, eventually she was employed in a small shop inside one of South Africa's hotels. Her hours 8.30 a.m. till five in the evening. But she became so excited about her new position she would stay on until the last customers were served. Today she is a partner in the business. She gave a lot and received a lot.

4. *Show the capacity to take responsibility*

Certainly the story above proved the value of this statement. Each can try to say where possible, can I have a go at whatever the challenge can be. I know it is not easy to stick ones neck out, in case we fail, but successful people have to take a chance and have a go. The more we endeavour to take on greater responsibility the more we are recognized as a person who can be trusted with a new task.

5. *Be tactful and polite*

Politeness goes hand in hand in "How to Win Friends and Influence People". I find in certain areas that politeness and courtesy has departed from our business scene. Why, I know not, because it takes no extra effort to say "Thank you" or "It's a pleasure", than to be sullen and uncaring.

When a person working in a shop shows kindness and interest in a customer there is a feeling of friendship between supplier and buyer.

This same attitude is most important when answering the telephone. A cheerful "good morning", the mentioning of the name of the company and "Can I help you", opens the door to a feeling of being wanted.

In business management we say the following:

The most important word is "You" — the second important word is we and the least is "I".

For example to say "Thank you for calling." "You are important to us". "You have made my day."

Then "We need you". "*We* are in business for *you*". "We are sorry we made a mistake."

Finally in relationship to "I". Again remember even if "I did not make the mistake" — this is used many times when a customer is complaining about an error in some direction or another. The member of the staff represents the company. So it should be easy to say: "We will put it right".

A tactful way of saying things often avoids a quarrel.

6. *Don't be a grouser*

Most of us grumble some time or another. But as a habit grumbling is a very unhealthy habit, as well as a hindrance in our career.

Nobody wants to give responsibility to a person who is forever moaning about something. No employer will want to promote a grouser, because it would have an adverse effect on the rest of the staff.

A person of strong character knows when to complain, but chooses the right time and place and to the right person.

We all know of people in offices, shops and other places of business who continue to gripe about nearly every situation. This causes a tense situation and can even cause dissention. What is more it lowers the morale of the firm and the efficiency suffers.

Dr Smiley Blanton wrote:

"Men and women need more than a salary to make life worthwhile. When work is not a source of personal satisfaction, it fails to serve as a proper outlet for our aggressive energy. That is why so many of us go through our jobs with a sense of futility or depression. That is partly the reason, too, for the widespread symptoms of anxiety so characteristic of modern times."

7. *Set out to please the people you serve*

A factor sometime forgotten—is that service is the key to a successful career. It must be remembered that although we intend to please our employer or boss, it is the client or customer who in the long run pays our salaries.

I was invited to address general managers of one of our largest hotel groups. Sitting next to me was the dynamic leader of the company. I opened my talk by saying "You are not employed to please the head of the company but to please the customers who pay your salaries and his as well." The man so well known in South Africa and overseas rose immediately and said "What you have said is the most important statement you can ever make."

Of course it is necessary to please your employer in order to conform with company policy, otherwise there can be confusion instead of harmony. Also the boss knows too he can rely on you to carry out his policy. Go the extra mile, it pays dividends.

8. *Use your spare time wisely*

As great as it is to enjoy your work and give it all you have got whilst at work, there must be time allocated to relaxation and the fulfilment of a hobby. A hobby which can take your mind away from your business career plays a very important and necessary part in your success. Our spare time should therefore be partly a time for refreshing our minds and bodies with new activities. It is also a time for rest and having moments of peace and quietness.

So many waste spare time with being bored and unhappy. The use of valuable time is essential to growth. This period can be used wisely to further our studies.

A POSITIVE REMINDER

Remind yourself several times daily, my attitudes are so important. At work and at home practice positive attitudes. See the reasons why you can do it, not the reason why you can't. Develop an "I'm winning" attitude. Put your intelligence to creative positive use. Use it to find ways to win—not to prove you will lose.

Find moments to reflect on how you deal with day to day situations. That is why use of spare time is so valuable.

9. *Take care of health*

In order to become successful in your "career"—health is so very vital. Without it we can only operate at a low percentage of our capability. Of course there are many who have achieved wonders, although suffering from ill-health. But where possible we must preserve God's great gift to us.

In our modern world much is made of keeping fit and we see men and women jogging, at gymnasiums and other centres to keep on top. But let us not lose sight of the fact that with all these helps to keeping the body in some form of shape, the mind plays an even greater role. Put it under pressure and all is well—place it under stress and then the problems start. That is why I said "use your spare time wisely". Relaxation stops the stress factor taking a hold.

If you feel low in spirit, first of all consult your medical doctor, this is truly a vital necessity. If all is well in this section of your life, then ask yourself am I happy in my work and if married is this working out alright. You will soon fasten on the reason for feeling down. I know I am dealing with many who consult me with the "low feeling" symptom.

A good tonic is laughter.

10. *Seize the opportunity*

One day the golden opportunity comes. The right job falls vacant; the time is ripe to ask for an increase of salary; this is the moment—take the opportunity!

You must not be afraid of what the opportunity may mean. Extra work, longer hours and many other areas which will be disrupted. That is if you are fully prepared for a change in many directions.

Opportunities often come disguised as difficulties; certainly they come as challenges. But if a new career demands greater effort—you can apply it.

One point does arise here. It is not everyone who wishes to be ambitious. Responsibility makes them unhappy, they are satisfied with what they are doing and they have enough money for their needs.

There is no reason why such a person should force himself to be ambitious. Not everyone can be at the top, and some are far happier in a job that does not demand too much of them.

Wisdom is to know what we want and to seek it by the right means that fits our personality.

The person who wants more than anything else to succeed in a career, to have an important job and to be at the top of the tree, should remember the African proverb

"Follow the bees, if you want to eat honey".

He or she should do everything possible to prepare for an opportunity, and when it appears seize it firmly.

No one ever reached the top of a tree by sawing off the branch on which he was sitting. The way to the top is by climbing, with all our skill, strength and persistence.

Great success to you!

---

15 *Why do we fear?*

The greatest obstacle to human progress is fear. We all know how it affects our lives.

Fear leaves the mind negative rather than positive, passive rather than active.

Think of the multitudes everywhere who are continually living in the shadow of fear. Fear appears to be everywhere! Fear of want, fear of starvation, fear of other's opinions, fear of what we won today may not be ours tomorrow, fear of sickness, fear of death. Fear has become with many, a fixed habit.

How are we to achieve mastery over this problem? It could be by the common method of seeking to conquer one by one all these strange fears that haunt us.

Dr Randall suggests we can clear up most of these fears by understanding. Most of us seem to accept fears of one sort or another as a basic way of life. When we ask is it really necessary to adopt this pattern of thinking, then we are on the road to a better way of living. The victim of fear or worry concerns himself or herself with a hundred things every day and night that there is not the slightest reason for being concerned about at all.

It is this victory over the root cause of every fear that we all need to gain. We have to banish all fear and distrust of life; we must confront each day in the attitude of confidence and courage. We have to dare ourselves to do it!

We human beings are fearful and worried because we do not think deeply enough into the meaning of life.

To affirm daily and persistently: "I know that I have

nothing to fear", will lead at length to that deep feeling within where "perfect love has cast out all fear".

I know it is not easy to do or maybe accept, but surely we all want to be as joyful, happy and successful as possible. We cannot have any of these positive attitudes if we are eaten up by fear.

Amazing how we all seem to cope with big problems or challenges, whilst the little ones fill us with doubt and worry. It must be that when we are faced with a mammoth task we call on all our abilities to deal with the situation. But the small problems we do not tackle maybe because they appear at the time to be insignificant.

There are thousands of people in this country today who have splendid ambitions, but who are so filled with doubt they never get started. Just waiting for a miracle to happen to restore the faith in themselves. So many will not burn the bridges behind them so as to commit themselves to their ambition and desires.

At the very outset of your career it is a splendid thing to make up your mind that you are going to cope with life in a positive way. That all hurdles you face are not stumbling blocks but stepping stones to greater achievements.

Confidence, self assurance, self faith—these are the great friends which help you to overcome fears and doubts.

Fear and lack of faith go hand in hand. The one is born of the other. Tell me how much one is given to fear, and I will tell you how much he lacks in faith. Fear is a most exclusive guest to entertain, the same as worry is. So expensive that none of us can afford to entertain them. We invite what we fear, the same as, by a different attitude of mind, we invite and attract the influences and conditions we desire. The mind dominated by fear opens the door to allow in the very things we don't want.

There is an old story relating to fear: "Where are you going?" asked an Eastern Pilgrim on meeting the "Plague" one day. "I am going to Bagdad to kill five thousand people," was the reply. A few days later the same pilgrim met the "Plague" returning. "You told me you were going to Bagdad to kill five thousand people, but instead you killed fifty thousand." "No," said the Plague, "I killed only five thousand, as I told you I would, the others died of fright."

I find in the work I do that many who ask me to help them are always "preparing for the worst". What will happen if this or that should happen? Do you think I could live through it and so on. Basically they have no reason to make such statements as the problems are only an imagination.

As parents we should make certain that our children face up to day to day living. They should also be taught to deal with each challenge they encounter.

A young boy, an outstanding runner used to win the 100 yards and 220 yards races, both at his own school and also at inter-school sports. His future in the athletic field seemed to be assured. One day he fell and did not finish the race. From then on he never won another race until I was able to point out—he had won dozens of sprints prior to the fall, so he was the same boy who won and tripped—but he won many times—but only tripped once. His fear blinded him to the truth about his ability to run.

"James Allen wrote."

"He who has conquered doubt and fear has conquered failure."

100

Courage should be taught in the schools, because everything that men and women strive for—success and happiness—are dependant upon it. Also, it enhances tremendously the power of all the mental faculties. Courage compensates for many defects and weaknesses.

Quit fearing things that may never happen. Fill your mind with courage and hope, and confidence.

Do not wait until fear thoughts become stuck in your mind and your imagination. Do not dwell upon them. Apply the antidote instantly and the fear is despatched.

What is this antidote that helps solve the fear problem! "There is no problem or fear I cannot deal with. I have faith in God as God has faith in me."

Put this into action and the light will begin to shine in the once troubled mind. Then you can truly say I am free.

THE FEAR OF CRITICISM

The fear of criticism robs men or women of their initiative. Destroys their power of imagination, limit their individuality, takes away self-reliance, and does damage in numerous ways.

Parents often do their children irreparable injury by criticising them.

Criticism is the one form of service of which everyone has too much. Everyone has a stock of it which is handed out, freely, whether called for or not.

Employers who understand human nature, get the best out of their staff, not by criticism, but by constructive suggestion. Parents will surely get the same results with their children. Criticism will plant fear in the minds of people, or maybe resentment, but it will not build love or affection.

FEAR OF FAILURE

Many with an outstanding ability do not reach their potential because they are obsessed with the fear of failure.

I am reminded of two men who sat for their chartered accountant's final examination. Both failed three times. One had the strength of character to keep on keeping on until at the fourth attempt he passed. The second man said no way am I going to try again. Today he is unemployed and told me. If only I hadn't given up. Setback's we all have, but to give up when we are nearly "Home" is a tragedy.

"Keep trying and eventually you will succeed."

THE FEAR OF OLD AGE

One great challenge we all have to face is the fear of growing old. Yet why fear that which happens to all of us. The key is to enjoy all parts of life. Youth, middle age and beyond. To realise that to many, the years past sixty can be excitement—no problems with children, finding time to do the things we always wanted to do!

But many are at their best at what some call old age. Look for example, the late Winston Churchill became famous in his late sixties. President Ronald Reagan now is past seventy. The South African State President is seventy.

The solution is to have an active mind and enjoy each day to the full. Don't fear old age—enjoy it.

THE FEAR OF ILL HEALTH

How strange it is when men and women who are basically fit in mind and body begin to believe they will one day become physically ill. I have met many, who fear they will contact some disease as they grow older.

Why anticipate that which has not taken place will be inevitable. What I believe we have to do is to count our blessings each day, especially if we are feeling well. Let us learn to think healthy thoughts and our bodies will in most cases respond.

If we could only rid ourselves of imaginary troubles said Dr Marden "Our lives would be infinitely happier and healthier." Thus one of the greatest tasks in character-building is to eliminate and wipe out all the unnecessary fears we develop.

People who have done this have learned that happiness can be achieved.

Every time you feel a sense of fear you must change the negative pattern to a more courageous one. Shun the fearful thoughts and replace them with thoughts of harmony and happiness. If you do this you will soon find that your environment will begin to change. Hope will brighten, you will have a healthier outlook upon life.

In overcoming your various fears, follow each one out to its logical conclusion and convince yourself that at the present moment the things you fear do not exist except in your imagination.

Merely convincing yourself that what you fear is imaginary will not work until you have trained your mind to throw off suggestions of fear, and to combat all thoughts that lead to it. This means you have to be watchful and alert to the all negative thoughts.

Whatever the means, the task of conquering fear is the most important in character-building. Not until this is done and done effectively can one say I now know how to live.

You can if you think you can!

16 *Let's have more cooperation this year*

If all of us could cooperate more than we do at present there would be greater harmony in this land.

I firmly believe that cooperation begins in the home. Benjamin Franklin the famous American said the following: "I noticed a mechanic, among a number of others, at work on a house a little way from my office, who always appeared to be in merry humour; he had a kind word and smile for everyone he met. Let the day be ever so cold, gloomy, or sunless, a happy smile danced on his cheerful fare. Meeting him one morning, I asked him to tell me the secret of his constant flow of happiness."

"It is no secret, doctor," he replied. "I have got one of the best of wives; and, when I go to work, she always has a kind word of encouragement for me; and when I go home, she meets me with a smile and a kiss; and she has done so many little things through the day to make me happy, that I cannot find it in my heart to speak an unkind word to anybody."

To the little child, home is his world—he knows no other. The fathers' love, the mothers smile all create a haven of joy and happiness.

MOST IMPORTANT WORD

An author tells the following story about a man whose seven sons were always quarrelling among themselves.

"One day he called them together and informed them that he wished to demonstrate just what their lack of cooperative effort meant. He had prepared a bundle of seven sticks which he carefully tied together. One by one he asked his sons to take the bundle and break it. Each son tried, but in vain. Then he cut the strings and handed one of the sticks to each of his sons and asked him to break it over his knee. After the sticks had all been broken, with ease, he said."

"When you boys work together in a spirit of harmony you resemble the bundle of sticks, and no one can defeat you; but when you quarrel among yourselves anyone can defeat you, one at a time."

There is a worthwhile lesson is this story and it may be applied to the people of a community—employees and employers in any business. It also applies to our nation.

Cooperation is said to be one of the most important words in the English language. So important is cooperation that no leader can do without it.

A Hindu Proverb:

"Help thy brothers' boat across the river and, lo! Thine own has reached the shore."

Success in this world is always a matter of individual effort, yet you will only be deceiving yourself if you believe that you can succeed without the cooperation of other people.

The value of friendships can never really be assessed. It is something that is so wonderful we are inclined to under-estimate what joy it can bring into our lives. If you cultivate attractive and lovable qualities, friends will flock around you.

Most of us are inclined to attend to everything else first, and if we find a little time we give this to our friends. Surely we ought to make a business of our friendships, they surely are worth it."

Do not be afraid to tell your friends that you care for them. Praise them for their kindness and consideration.

Always be ready to lend a hand.

Cooperation in married life makes for a happy union. A great deal has been said in a cynical way about the immense number of unhappy marriages. There is so much said on this subject that it is easy to forget that for every instance of complaint there are a far greater number of prosperous marriages of which we hear to little about.

Nowhere does it prove so true as in married life, that your happiness is found in giving love to your partner and in supporting each other. But there are no short cuts to happiness. Men and women who marry must acquire thoughtfulness, self-control, consideration for others, patience and other such qualities that make for harmonious cooperation.

A husband should continue through life the same tenderness that in youth gained the affections of his wife. Devote yourself to her, and after the hours of business enjoy her company, appreciate her and tell her so.

Today with so many wives working it is still important that she finds time to share her love and thoughts with her husband when she too returns from work.

What a man desires in a wife is her companionship sympathy and love. Put it all together and it means cooperation.

Now let us look at cooperation in business-starting with employer—employee relationship.

Employers today have to rely on their staff. The employers cannot succeed alone, no matter how great their ability may be. The most progressive employers look upon their employees as partners.

Business men and women have found out—some the hard way—that there is a tremendous loss of productiveness because employer and employee do not pull together. If the employers and employees would work closer together there would be such a vast increase in production that the inflation rate would drop.

A chain is only as strong as it's weakness link. Therefore it can be said that a manager is only as strong as the people working for him or her.

A manager obtains his results through the efforts of the people working for him. His basic job is therefore to develop his staff to be able to achieve greater performance.

If a manager is to get the highest results from his team he must understand what their personal aims are.

I have watched a large retail company lose staff because the leader has not found time to communicate with her staff. The lack of cooperation has held back the development of this company.

In motivating people it is important for the manager to treat his/her staff according to their personal makeup.

No two are alike, and no two respond exactly alike to the same treatment. The leader must get close to the team, understanding them and giving encouragement at all times.

Now the employee has to ask what am I prepared to contribute—asking maybe the following questions.

(a) What is the most important contribution I can make to the performance of the company.
(b) What self development do I need.

(c) What standards do I have to set myself.

So now it is apparent that cooperation is needed from leader to staff and staff to leader.

There is a poem which really sums up what working together means.

IF I WERE BOSS

If I were boss I would like to say: You did a good job here today. I'd look for a man, or girl or boy whose heart would leap with a thrill of joy at a word of praise, and I'd pass it out where the crowd could hear as I walked about.

If I were Boss I would like to find the fellow whose work is the proper kind; and whenever to me a good thing came I'd like to be told the toiler's name, and I'd go to him, and I'd pat his back, and I'd say "That was perfectly spendid, Jack."

Now a bit of praise isn't much to give but it's dear to the hearts of all that live; and there's never a man on this good old earth but is glad to be told when he's been of worth; is welcome and wanted everywhere.

If I were boss I'm sure I would say a kindly word whenever I could for a man who has given his best by day wants a little more than his weekly pay, he likes to know with the setting sun that the boss is pleased with the work he's done.

When we refer to cooperation it must be remembered that supplier to customer attitude is vital. So often in these days little consideration is given to the customer. What is lacking is the service that one expects from the supplier. Promises on times of delivery have in many cases been broken. Maybe we can capture a new desire to have complete cooperation in all spheres of commerce. Let promises be kept and let us begin to give good value whether it be for services given or products sold. Cooperation will bring greater prosperity to all.

Finally as I close this chapter one of the most important functions for all of us to attend to is the cooperation between all peoples in South Africa. Let us declare right now that as people work together for harmony—peace and prosperity, greater understanding develops.

With greater cooperation we will see a new horizon bringing—joy—happiness and love to everyone living in this great land.

Cooperation—is a key to successful living

---

17 *Develop a winning attitude to life*

Ability alone is not enough to ensure success in one's career, one's social life, or with hobbies. To make best use of one's talents a self-confidence is needed which visualises success by making plans for it.

Put out of mind all fears of defeat. Expect victory, plan for victory. Build up a positive mental attitude to win. That is the spirit shown by those who never give up, who continue trying to do still better even when they have already achieved immense success.

The will to win can be developed by systematic practice. Try to think calmly without panic. Ask questions continually, for much of success depends on knowledge. Act as though success is certain, but not in a show-off conceited way.

Always give of your best, remembering that always means always. That will make your successes as big as they can possibly be, while your failures will be reduced in size. Be enthusiastic, behave towards everyone with the greatest courtesy, get into the do-it-now habit. Put fear behind you, have faith in your abilities. Aim high; be persistent in your efforts.

All these are ways to strengthen your will to win. Taken all at once, they sound a tall order. Fortunately, there are ways to help you in creating the winning attitude.

In the United States a survey was carried out to find what was the most important formula of success. The university involved broke it down under four headings: (a) IQs. (b) Knowledge. (c) Skills. (d) Attitudes. It was found that although the first three were vital, attitude was the real reason of success. For without the right mental attitude the other three are not used to their fullest extent.

So first of all get your attitude to life right then you can put all your know-hows into action.

Now begin to develop your talents. Make as much as you possibly can of your abilities. That means you must be able to recognise what your talents are, a task which is less easy than it may sound.

Many a person has discovered fairly late in life where their true talents lie. Often we say of a person that he or she has missed their vocation, with the meaning that they have exceptional ability in a field of effort different from that to which they have devoted themselves.

Discover your true talents by searching-self-analysis. What are your favourite activites? What tasks do you prefer in your day's work? What sort of books do you read? What subjects do you mainly discuss with your friends? Bit by bit you can put together a picture of yourself which will enable you to see where your true abilities lie.

When you are sure you have recognised your talents, do all in your power to develop them.

A winning attitude to life is a characteristic of the initiators, the people who start things. Initiative may be acquired by those with the courage to speak up. Do not remain silent or inactive when you see something that needs doing. Do not wait for someone else to do it, or to tell you to do so.

Initiative is largely a question of will power. You must have the determination not only to seize opportunities when they appear but to create them.

When an opportunity has arisen or has been created act

at once. Do-it-now is the key motto of those with the winning attitude. Hesitation, doubt, procrastination are the hall-marks of people who fear failure. By their fears they create failure because their action, when at last it takes place, is half-hearted.

Be bold, act with confidence. More often than not you will succeed. On the few occasions when you fail, put it down to experience, then start afresh. Do not allow a past failure to deter you from your goal.

Keep your conversation positive. Talk about all the reasons why you can succeed. Avoid all thoughts of why you can't cope. Keeping your mind fixed on the positive reasons why success is likely, you condition yourself for success thus making it possible that things will work out as you wish. Your performance, the use you make of your abilities, is determined by your mental outlook more than by anything else.

Enthusiasm is vital. It comes largely from knowing exactly what it is you want. Keep firmly in your mind a clear picture of your goal or goals. Let all your thoughts, all your actions, be directed towards achieving them. Act enthusiastically, even if in the most, trying and difficult situations. You will find that such actions inevitably generates enthusiasm.

A winning attitude involves organisation. You must plan your days. Do not allow time to drift by as you try one thing after another, really not knowing where you are going. When circumstances make you alter your plan through reasons which you have to accept, then make a fresh plan immediately. For example a young man at university studying law, loses his father. He has to change his whole life style as his mother is unable to support him. Maybe he

113

has to leave university and take a job. His new plan could be to support himself, but now to study by correspondence to complete his career to become a lawyer.

Perseverance is essential. Few worthwhile things are achieved easily or without setbacks. It is when things go wrong that your winning attitude best reveals itself as you now have to adjust and fight back.

People who lack a winning attitude are never at loss for excuses for their failures. Many methods exist whereby they manage to hide from themselves the truth about their failure. All these methods come from taking a negative defeatist attitude. The first of these excuses consists of the idea that you were far too busy doing something else. Mostly something far less important.

The second might be described as safety first. Hesitation, procrastination, lack of courage to take decisive action may all be explained away. Always waiting one believes for the right moment to set the wheels into action.

The third method is over-concentration on one aspect of life. A commitment which take up all your time and provides an excuse for avoiding all other activities. For example an aged parent who need looking after is often turned into a noble reason for side-stepping the challenges of marriage.

The last of the four main ways of evading positive living is to retreat into helplessness "The I'm no good at that sort of thing" attitude. This person belongs to the P.L.O.M. Club. "The poor little old me approach". Many people I know have joined this club for years and even become life members.

The way to beat these negative thoughts is to act as though you will become a winner. In other words, keep your mind away from the reasons why you think you will fail, in order to concentrate it instead on positive facts that will help you succeed.

A person with a winning attitude is using the mind all the time to make improvements, to find new ways of doing things. He or she uses the imagination creatively to reach out to greater horizons. These dynamic people take nothing for granted, looking all the while for better ways to complete a task and reach a goal. They know only too well that ideas are the foundation of all progress.

By this method positive people do not fall into a rut. They are always seeking to improve their lives and by so doing help others to do the same.

Finally to sum up, the methods suggested are as follows:

(1) Develop the will to win. Expect victory, do not fear defeat.
(2) Recognize your talents. Cultivate them fully.
(3) Create opportunities, build up initiative, generate enthusiasm, by the do it now habit.
(4) Organize your time. Persevere in face of set-backs.
(5) Replace negative opinions with positive facts.
(6) Keep out of the rut by using your creative imagination.

A poem which has helped many is this one:

ALL IN THE STATE OF THE MIND

If you think you are beaten, you are.
If you think you dare not, you don't.
If you would like to win, but think you can't
Its almost a cinch you won't.
If you think you'll lose, you're lost,

Living your life

For out in the world you find
Success begins with a fellow's will.
It's all in the state of the mind.

For many a race is lost
Ere ever a step is run;
and many a coward fails
Ere ever his works begun.
Think big and your deeds will grow.
Think small and you'll fall behind;
Think that you can and you will.
It's all in the state of the mind.

If you think you are outclassed you are;
You got to think big to rise,
You have got to be sure of yourself before
You can ever win a prize.
Life's battles don't always go
To the stronger or faster man,
But sooner or later the man who wins
Is the man who thinks he can.

116

18 *Possessiveness*

The dictionary describes posessiveness as follows: "Extreme attachment to one's possessions; desire to dominate another emotionally." It is the latter which I find so prevalent in the counselling work I do to assist people.

There are five categories I would like to refer to, although no doubt you may find many more.

(1) Marriage.
(2) Children.
(3) Parents and in-laws.
(4) When a husband/wife dies.
(5) Single parent.

(1) *Marriage*

Many cases we hear or read about relate to one of the partners endeavouring to dominate the other, causing disharmony and eventually unhappiness. It appears that the male in most cases is the villain of the story (although I can cite many wives who dominate their husbands). Let it be said that countless women allow their men to run the home and make all decisions thus taking away their own individuality and suppressing their personality. But for a male to totally possess his wife in all aspects of her life so much so that in the end she becomes a shadow of the woman he married and only an echo of his demands.

Jealousy is one area where possessiveness makes for unhappiness. A woman told me that it is useless for her to go out to dinner or to a dance with her husband and friends, because always on the way home "he calls me a trollip, accusing me of eyeing all the men present". He tells her he loves her so much, he cannot do without her. But the woman is so completely miserable. "I love him, but cannot take anymore of his jealousy."

As I sight this particular case, I asked the woman in question: "Was your husband like this before you married." "Yes," she said "in reflection he was, but I thought he loved me so much—it never occurred to me how jealous he really was."

I believe that if in courting or in early marriage it becomes apparent that jealousy has started—then the problem has to be dealt with immediately. It must not be left as the problem will not take care of itself.

In an opposite case a woman blamed her husband of having affairs with all the women at his office. "She would call or telephone me just to see what I could be up to." In this particular marriage, the husband said to me—"She is so possessive I dare not even mention how attractive an actress was in the movies, else she would sulk or nag." The marriage broke up. Jealousy is a killer of love. It can never bring joy into a home. It destroys affection. To possess is to own, and in marriage no one must possess the other. To share, to discuss, to be truthful, honest and giving is the freedom of our individuality and the hallmark of a successful union.

(2) *Children*

An enormous problem is how parents and in most cases the mother possess the child or children. A lone child is more susceptible to being affected by an over-protective mother than if he or she had brothers and sisters.

Possessiveness

When a child is young it obviously relies on the parent for security. Meaning to be cared for and loved. But if as it develops the child cannot begin to form opinions, or friendships without the mother saying "Your mother knows best"—and implies if the child disagrees with her, she becomes upset, so much so that the youngster accepts what the mother wants, thus starting a pattern which can continue not only during the early years but into adolescence and even beyond.

Possessive parents really believe they love their children that they have to protect them from all of life's challenges. But there is another form of possessiveness that I have to refer to. The running of the lives of the children to such an extent the youngsters are placed under extreme pressures. It is true to some extent, says the experts, that children have to learn to live under limited pressure. But it is important to differentiate between what is necessary and what is not. A child must learn to get to school on time, to develop good manners and to get along with other children. These are within the child's capacity at one stage of growth or another. But it is when we place him under abnormal pressures—to be brilliant beyond his capacities, to be a leader when he is not ready for leadership—that he is going to have difficulties.

Some parents ask a child to compete with an impossible ideal. "We want *our* child to be better than the rest and we intend to see he or she does just that.

Children learn early that success wins aclaim and failure invites reproach. The child who cannot constantly measure up to his parent's expectations rapidly begins to lose his self confidence, to lose the feelings of self-worth that enables a mature adult to face life with vigour.

Although there is no set rule by which parents can cope with the challenges pushing their children prematurely into an adult world, there are a few commonplace guides:

Try to differentiate between the normal pressures that should be placed on children and the excessive pressures that may be only a reflection of inflated parental ambitions.

Find out exactly how many demands are being made on your child's time, and if he or she is overburdened help them cut down some things that are not so important.

Most important, a child must know that he is loved for himself, even though he cannot compete with others.

(3) *Parents/Inlaws*

Over a period of years I have been asked to help young couples to try and find a solution relating to possessive parents who believe they must assist the newly weds in aspects of married life. In many cases the mother of the son feels she can show the new bride how to take care of her son, the way he had been used to. Of course the mother means well. But once children leave home to map out their own lives, parents must only help when called upon for advice. Otherwise conflicts develop and it places either the young man or young woman under terrific pressure, as they do not want to hurt the parents.

Many marriages break-up due to this major problem.

I have suggested to most couples who have come for marriage guidance to sit down with their parents before they are married and discuss openly "with love," their feeling about what they want to do as they start their new life together. Asking the parents to let them work out their own ideas in the very new experience. Saying they will seek advice when it is needed.

The young bride has her own ideas of what she wants in the home and how to look after her man. The husband who may well have been spoilt whilst living with his parents, has to learn to adjust. This can only be done when there is no outside interference.

Another form of possessiveness comes to light when the parents expect the children to be with them every Sunday, and become upset if this does not happen. It is even more aggravated when babies appear on the scene and the grandparents must see them each weekend. Again this is only natural but if their is a strong love between parents and their children a beautiful arrangement can be arrived to the joy of all parties.

Possessiveness drives a wedge into happiness—whilst caring love opens doors.

(4) *When a husband/wife dies*

An enormous burden is placed on the surviving spouse not only to earn a living but how to deal with a child or children. I am referring to a relatively young person say in the thirty's who is now alone. The loss of a loved one is so difficult to bear. But to the parent still living—life has to go on.

This can be the start of a child being looked upon as someone not only to be cared for but for the child to take place of the mother or father who has died. If one is not careful, possessiveness now becomes apparent.

In a case study, a father died leaving the mother and a son of 15 to cope with life. In no time the mother expected the son to take the place of the father. After school the boy had to come home do his homework and carry out certain duties which his late father had done. Then at week-ends the mother expected the son to be with her virtually all the time. At first for the first year the boy accepted this as he loved his mother dearly. But he wanted to spend time with his friends and continue with his sport. The mother felt he was selfish and didn't love her.

I explained that her son had a right to pursue his own life and further more he loved her dearly and also missed his dad so very much.

Now the relationship is fine, she no longer possesses him, but has found friends of her own.

In another incident a father left alone, relied upon his daughter to cook, sew and do much around the home. Still at school in matric, the girl found she could not cope. She gave up ballet, but when she came to me, she was bordering on a breakdown. After her visit to her medical doctor, who advised her to talk out her problem with her father, the two of them spent time with me discussing what could be done to correct the problems. The daughter loved her dad so much she wanted to always please him. The father at loss on how to cope with his life, failed to notice the daughter was rundown.

He was in his own way possessing his daughter, without realizing it.

(5) *Single parent*

Either by death or divorce we find many, many single parents coping with bringing up children. If a normal relationship takes place that is great, but there are numerous situations where the parent holds on to the child or children, frightened to let them experience their own adventures. To possess by fear is a habit that must be released immediately.

122

Possessiveness

The single parent is faced with many challenges, having to deal with financial, emotional and health problems. This places them under enormous pressure. They must not blame the children for these situations and at the same time allow the boy or girl to live a normal life and certainly not to become too possessive that the children are in bondage to the single parent.

Finally there are many other pitfalls that relate to possessiveness, but I have tried to show the reader some aspects they have to watch out for.

The more you let go of your loved one, the more they will love you.

19 *26 Ways to success*

I have chosen the alphabet for a success pattern. Each letter has a positive formula. I have divided the 26 ways to success in two parts. This chapter A–M.

A *Attitude*

Your attitude to situations will determine your growth. Your attitude will shape your future. That is why a positive mental attitude is needed. As an example, think back on the men's tennis final at Wimbledon. Boris Becker said before the match, I will win again, because I am at my best playing on a grass court. Ivan Lendl said to play on grass was a problem for him as he cannot succeed on a grass court. Well we all know who won—Lendl the No. 1 in the world talked himself out of winning—Boris Becker used the P.M.A. method and won.

Get the positive thinking right and you are on the way to success. Of course it means effort, determination and practice. Many fail because of a negative approach to a situation. A young student will say I won't pass my exam's, helping the failure pattern to move into the subconscious mind. Whilst another will say I will try and do my best. Whatever the result—the "I can principle" stimulates you—the "I can't" depletes your efforts.

> ## Your attitude determines your life

B *Belief*

One of the great tragedies in our modern world is the question "Do I really believe". Many say of course, "For I believe in God". But how big is that belief? For in my work many outstanding men, women, boys and girls come for advice. When asked, Do you honestly believe in God? You see a kind of doubt on the faces. Not that they don't want to believe, but something has happened in their lives which caused a doubt. Like "my marriage is on the rocks" or "I can't find a job"—or "nobody cares for me." You see how little do we believe when things go wrong. Remembering— you have to also believe in yourself. This is a key to many who succeeded. Not just the ability or education, but the belief in the "I can do it" attitude.

> **So believe to succeed**

C *Commitment*

Success will only come when you are committed to some cause. Whether it be marriage, a profession, business or whatever, a commitment is necessary. You then develop a positive habit. "Sow an action and you reap a habit; sow a habit and you reap a character! Sow a character and you reap a destiny." So said the great American psychologist Dr. William James. He was saying you are what you have totally committed yourself to. Become a self-starter.

Whatever job you do, give of your best, so many only give what they are paid to do. If you are truly committed you will satisfy yourself. Your own efforts will eventually bring the rewards.

The outstanding sportsmen and women are totally aware of their commitments to the goals they have chosen!

Have you a firm commitment?

D *Dare*

Take one of your problems and decide you are going to overcome it. Work for a whole week on this challenge. Write down your problem and next to it put what you believe could be the solution. Each day review your thoughts and soon you will be dwelling only on the positive answer.

Recently a young married couple came to see me, as their marriage was beginning to sour. After the first consultation we were able to arrive at the problem. This may sound humorous as I tell you what caused the problem, but to the wife especially, it was extremely serious. She could not stand the way her husband would eat his food. He apparently made unpleasant noises which irritated her no end. But it was only at the end of our first meeting that she opened up and told her husband what was the cause of her being unhappy. The husband, amazed, said why didn't you tell me before. The reply: I felt if I did, it would hurt you. You see how little things in life can cause a big upset.

I dare you to sort out your problems

E *Enthusiasm*

Do you want to feel enthusiastic—"yes" I am sure you would reply. Then learn this self motivation phrase:

To be enthusiastic act enthusiastic. What is the key word? ACT. What ever we want to be, we have to act the part. Enthusiasm is contagious, it rubs off on others we meet or work with. Watch how a child acts with enthusiasm. We just become carried away with his or her excitement.

To be enthusiastic is a key to happiness. So few these days seem to find living a joy.

> ## So do it now: act enthusiastically

F *Forgiveness*

Is there someone in your family or circle of friends who has upset you. Then, please, forgive them immediately. Little do we know what we do to ourselves when we harbour a grudge. It causes us to only see the worst in the person who we feel has been the reason for our hurt. Sometimes we all say things to each other that is hurtful, but we have to learn to ask forgiveness. It usually clears the air. If someone has said something to us which stings, then ask straight away, does he or she mean it. Act immediately and forgive them. Instead of letting the hurt fester, forgive and you release the tension.

Forgiveness is an important part of love. When we truly love it is so much easier to forgive. Jesus taught us to forgive our enemies.

127

> ## If there is someone to forgive: Do it now

G *Giving*

To give of yourself is the start of a full and successful life.
Please read the following which to me shows the true art of giving.

IF

If you do your best and always try to fulfill the responsibility with which you are entrusted.

If you keep clean in thought and body—if you exemplify clean habits, clean speech, clean sport.

If you have the courage to face danger in spite of fear.

If you work faithfully and make the best of your opportunities.

If you are a friend to all and a brother to every living man.

If you are polite to all, especially to the weak, helpless, and unfortunate.

If you smile when you can, do your work promptly and cheerfully—and if you never shirk or grumble at responsibilities or hardships.

If you are loyal to all to whom loyalty is due, to the members of your family, the firm you work for and your country.

If you do your best to do your duty to God and your country. To help others at all times, to keep yourself physically strong, mentally awake and morally straight.

Then you live by the law of giving and by the right standards.

That which you share will multiply

H *Hope*

Hope is holding on, it is never giving up. It is never quitting.

Hope is the start of trusting, it is the belief that prayer does work.

Hope is to expect good things to happen. It is the road toward your goals.

Try and develop a pattern of belief. The person hopes to find the job. A child hopes to pass the examination. You hope for better things to come into your life. With hope it helps you to success.

Hope and trust are the targets to live by

I *Imagination*

One of the greatest gifts you were given, is the power of imagination. Outstanding sportsmen and women use it constantly. The idea is to see yourself achieving success in your imagination before you go into action and begin to actually work towards your goal. You visualize the end result in your subconscious mind. Then by storing the

129

thought in your mind you are in fact starting to accomplish your goal.

An example is of a golfer who before he starts his round, sees himself playing each hole in his imagination. This prepares him for the actual playing of the round and fills his mind with success.

Young people at school can practise this method before sitting for examinations. I have shown many children how to put this into action, with outstanding results.

Sit quietly down and let your imagination begin to work for you. When an idea comes write it down. You will be surprised at the results you will achieve.

Remember that imagination is a gold mine

J *Joy*

Begin each day with joy in your heart. Even though you may be facing difficulties. When you feel good about something you have done, you become joyful. Let this feeling be with you as much as possible, for you begin to radiate happiness and all around you pick up this wonderful experience. Be aware what joy can do for you. You see things through the eyes of fulfilment. Physically, mentally and spiritually you relate to a new design for living.

Today experience joy

K *Kindness*

This covers many facets of day to day living. Kindness is to be thoughtful—caring—considerate—understanding. One special way is always to be kind to those who work for you or under your direction. A caring boss is always looked up to, and what is more he or she gets far more out of the staff. Courtesy is another form of kindness. In many ways it is sadly lacking in our modern version of living. We sometimes forget to be polite to each other. This is very apparent in the way we drive our motor-cars.

To be considerate is really a form of loving one another. It means we are thoughtful and caring.

Kindness is love in action

L *Laughter*

This is music to the soul and so contagious that many who are feeling low in spirit, pick up the vibes and begin to join in the happiness that is engulfing them.

I have learned one secret when I give a lecture or an after dinner talk—that is to try and make the audience laugh. You watch them grin—giggle—chuckle then fold-up. Immediately, they become relaxed and at ease. This same principle applies to business and especially family life. Where there is humour you find happiness. Where there is laughter you find love.

Laugh and the world laughs with you

131

M *Manage*

To be successful in any profession we must give complete attention to details. It is an element of effectiveness, which if we are to manage our lives we cannot ignore.

To manage time is an important factor in our day to day living. Waste not time, for we can never use what has been lost.

If we can save a single hour, in a normal life time—one hour saved each day of a five day week is worth six years of productive effort.

Whatever time we save can be used for self-improvement, by study, lectures or reading.

We must learn to manage our affairs. Communication—relationship and our money.

To learn the art of communication is a science in itself. By practice and effort, we can succeed. Our relationships are important so we must not lose sight of how we manage to relate to each other. Finally to manage our finances is an important function of stability in our affairs. It is said that we should always save 10% of our salary. It is not easy but let us try!

Manage your life—it is important to you

---

20 *26 Ways to success*

PART 2

N *Need*

Everyone in the world must have a need and to be needed. To have a need is really a setting of a goal. All must strive for something. It is a spurt to success and fulfilment. Many battle through life because they believe they are not needed.

All of us must find a need and explore it. Great ideas develop when we search for what is needed by people. New inventions or discoveries materialize when we find a new way to do things.

But the greatest and most important of all is to be wanted by others. Many hurts and sufferings can be put aside when someone says "I need you".

> **So today tell someone "You need them"**

O *Organize*

The need to plan your affairs as efficiently as possible is a necessity in coping with all facets of life. This does not mean we are so organized that life becomes dull and lacks adventure. But we surely must follow basics, such as an organized home, for this makes for a feeling of security especially if we are married with children. Certain routines are a must. Good habits are created by all concerned, when there is a family plan for living.

The organized student is the one who has a better chance of passing an examination than the boy or girl who muddles along and there is no planned study programme.

Organized effort is a driving force we all need. That is why all must enjoy work.

Miss Alma-Tadena, in her lecture on "What is Happiness?" said it took her five months to write down the definition of happiness. She says that happiness is the result of working hard and developing one's powers to the limit. She does not believe that it is possible for a person to be very happy while he or she is conscious that they are developing only a small percentage of their ability.

> **Organized effort will produce more work and of a better quality than is possible without it**

P *Persevere*

It is only by reflection that we derive a just appreciation of the value of perseverance. When we see how much can be accomplished in any given direction by the man or woman of but average ability who resolutely perseveres in the course of action adopted as the ruling purpose of their lives, we then arrive at a just estimate of the value of perseverance as a factor in success.

In all activities of life the boy or girl, man or woman will reach their goals by sticking to the task on hand, until they complete what was started. So many fall by the wayside, because they give up, half way to their original goal.

I have watched outstanding scholars whilst at school do little with their abilities when they move into the business world because they do not motivate themselves. It is by keeping on that the victory is won.

Learn to carry a thing through to its conclusion. Then it can be said—"I have reached a goal."

Be persistent to achieve enduring success

Q *Quit*

Why do I say quit, when this appears to be giving up—I mean quit complaining! Quit seeing the worst in certain situations! Quit finding fault with other people and look for the good in them. Quit running away from life and learn to deal with challenges.

Here is a poem written years ago—the author unknown but it really is so true.

DON'T QUIT

When things go wrong as they sometimes will,
When the road you are trudging seems all uphill,
When funds are low and the debts are high,
And you want to smile but you had to sigh,
When care is pressing you down a bit,
Rest if you must, but don't you quit.

Life is queer with its twists and turns,
As everyone sometimes learn,
And many a failure turns about,
When he might have won had he stuck it out.
Don't give up, though the pace seems slow—
You may succeed with another blow.

Often the goal is nearer than
it seems to a faint and
struggling man.
Often the struggler has given up,
when he might have captured the victor's cup.
And he learned too late when the night slipped down,
how close he was to the golden crown.

Success is failure turned inside out—
The silver tent of the clouds of doubt,
And you never can tell how close you are,
It may be near when it seems afar—
So stick to the fight when you're hardest hit—
It's when things seem worst that you musn't quit.

"So keep on keeping on"

R   *Resolute determination*

We find that everything that happens in this world is
brought about by faith. If it were not for faith and trust
little would be accomplished. Faith then is the keynote of
knowing that we have the determination to cope with day
to day living.

If you give yourself a challenge you are more likely to
accomplish all you would like to do. Say to yourself
something like this "this may be difficult, and it may be
hard to complete what I have in mind for the morning, but
I am going to prove I can do it". It really is putting your
shoulders back and demanding of yourself you can cope
with this situation.

Once you resolve that you are going to do this it appears
as though there is something that is pushing you swiftly
from one task to another.

The practice of setting yourself a goal, you will find helpful in coping with life. Determination will give you added courage to succeed.

Today determine your future

S *Service*

When you look at the successes of great women and men they have in some way helped others as they advance themselves.

One of the greatest attitudes in life is to give. Does this sound crazy? Well lets look at this point.

I am offered a job, it appears to be ineffective with little prospect. So I just linger along, do what I have to do and no more. Then say "I told you so—no future prospects so why should I push myself?

Now the giver is the one who accepts the position with enthusiasm and is thankful he or she has a job. Right at the beginning it is decided to do what you have to do—then look for more work. The one who is serving is excited about learning new ideas and techniques, thus improving his or her knowledge and at the same time helping others. This person is soon noticed and with it follows promotion.

Your attitude determines your result

T *Tact*

One who is tactful has a keen sense of saying and doing the right thing at the right time, and in so doing avoids offending others. Tactful persons are said to be diplomatic. Someone has said "the secret of all success lies in being alive to what is going on around you; in adjusting oneself to the present surroundings; in being sympathetic and helpful; in knowing what is wanted at the time; in saying to others what they want to hear at the right moment".

What we all have to do is to remember that there are millions of different human opinions, of which our own is but one. Remembering that tact is to have the ability to put yourself in the other persons place and to consider the matter as it appears to him.

Tact wins friends

U *Understanding*

Understanding and tolerance are traits which appear to be forgotten by many. It has been suggested that "Tolerance is open-mindedness on all subjects". It is not a willingness to change our own opinions but rather recognition of the rights of others to have their own opinions.

We all should work harder to understand other people and to find out why they think the way they do.

It is well to remember that the opinions held by our friends and neighbours might be right and our own could be wrong.

Let us remember that no two of us are identical. We all have the right to think and plan, and so has the other person.

With understanding—a better world

V *Victory*

The secret of successful living is to be found in training the mind, training the will and developing the right attitudes. Of course these three are interlocked. Attention to one inevitably helps the others. Whilst neglecting one will hinder all three. So do not expect quick results from your programme for more successful living you cannot secure sudden, miraculous results. All the same, once you make a serious start, progress should soon be noticeable and continue fast enough to give you incentive to carry on.

Begin with two goals to help you train your mind. The first of these is concentration. Learn to concentrate by starting jobs instead of thinking about starting them.

Concentration is a goal you can achieve by maximising your efforts and minimising distractions.

The next target is training your mind in memory.

Remember there is no reason at all why anyone should have a bad memory if they really want a good one, but the solution to all this training is by application every day.

The following are a few simple rules which will assist you to improve your memory.

(1) Be interested in what you want to remember.
(2) Link the new knowledge to the old.
(3) Divide your study-time into short periods.
(4) Write down thoughts and ideas.
(5) Keep learning all the time.

Victory is yours right now

W *Work*

There is no substitute for work. This is the only way we can develop. When we enjoy what we do there is a marked improvement in our attitude towards others. In addition we feel fitter physically. Having a purpose in life helps us to feel needed. Work well done gives us a satisfaction we cannot find elsewhere.

When we find a job that brings us satisfaction life around us seems so different.

Do whatever you are doing with love in your heart and life will have a special meaning for all concerned.

Work is life's fulfillment

X *X-ray*

Whatever our motives in whatever we are doing lets X-ray our minds to make sure that our motives are right.

Sometimes when we do this we see ourselves in a new light. Often we don't like what we see because we have been kidding ourselves and now the real motives are brought into view.

Ask yourself, what do I really want to accomplish, then ask yourself if I continue the way I am, will I achieve what I desire?

140

X-ray your thoughts and find who you really are

Y *You*

You are the most important person in your life. That is why you must learn to love yourself a lot more. Remembering that you have to learn to mind your own business as it is the most important business in your world.

You have much to do to find out your true identity and your potential.

You are great

Z *Zest*

When you see others happy, laughing and sincerely enjoying what they do—we say they have a zest for living.

What about you—are you on top of your job, living it and giving of your best. Do you only look forward to weekends? If so change your attitude. Weekenders have little zest for living as most of the week is a bind.

Be a seven day a week person and see how you grow!

Zest—Enjoyment in action

21 *The Spirit of Christmas*

With the tough economy which nearly all South Africans are experiencing, many are asking how will this effect Christmas.

Don't you think that this will give us the opportunity to examine the true meaning of Christmas.

Somewhere, along the way many of us have lost sight of the spirit of Christmas. Over many years this has developed into a materialistic festival. Gift swopping, parties, celebrations and many such activities.

Now, we can renew our vows of love which cost nothing, but gives much to many.

As this is a time of the year that relates to children let those who have toys aplenty and so often never played with give the surplus to needy children. Suggest to them, that they make a list of dolls and mechanical toys they don't really need. Place them in a box and then with the help of the parents take them to orphanages and personally give them away. To the child who is giving away his or her toys will come a new side of living. They will watch with joy and happiness the wonderful facial expression on the one receiving the present. I can assure you once this has been started the more fortunate children will look forward to Christmas as a time for sharing and better still caring. There are many associations which can help repair broken toys.

I remember years ago when our children were small and I was at that time singing in a church choir, some of the young boys in the choir came from either broken homes or had no parents, we seniors in the choir used to entertain these lads at Christmas time. It truly was a feeling of goodwill.

I know there are many kind and considerate persons who really do practise the spirit of Christmas. But maybe we could get the children and youth to express themselves individually.

Another way to help balance the family budget as the month of December is upon us, is for the Children not to buy Christmas cards, but to prepare and draw their own. This gives parents and friends alike the feeling of someone caring for them. Time taken with love preparing the cards is a joy in itself.

As far as we adults are concerned, let us, wherever possible, find some surplus clothing in our wardrobes, and pass them on to somebody who will be thankful to receive a gift. I bet we all have clothing, we haven't worn for years and yet believing we will one day be able to use the garment. Check the waste line? Sigh, smile and give the undersize away.

Yes Christmas, can be a wonderful time to take stock of all that we have, but at the same time never forgetting the less fortunate. What about a stocktaking of our attitudes to others during the past year. Maybe, some Christmas resolutions are needed. Such as forgiving someone who you believed has hurt you.

Send a Christmas card to a person who has slighted you. Yes! Love does find a way.

Perhaps the following thoughts could help each one of us.

TODAY

Mend a quarrel. Search out a forgotten friend. Dismiss suspicion and replace it with trust. Write a love letter. Share some treasure. Give a soft answer. Encourage youth. Manifest your loyalty in a word or deed. Keep a promise. Find the time. Forego a grudge. Forgive an enemy. Listen. Apologize, if you were wrong. Try to understand. Flout envy. Examine your demands on others. Think first of someone else. Appreciate, be kind. Be gentle. Laugh a little more.

Deserve confidence. Take up arms against malice. Decry complacency. Express your gratitude. Worship your God. Gladden the heart of a child. Take pleasure in the beauty and wonder of the earth. Speak your love. Speak it again. Speak it still again. Speak it still once again.

Author Unknown

If we could carry out the above beautiful thoughts Christmas would have its complete meaning. Jesus showed us that if we truly loved we had to forgive. Should we learn from this, then we could start a chain reaction throughout this land.

For many young people, the period prior to Christmas is the finishing of their school years. Ready to await with trepidation the results of the exams which they sat a few weeks before. But don't let the tension effect your appreciation of family life. Remembering the prayers, love and consideration your parents have given you throughout your school years.

Christmas could be a way of telling mum and dad how much they mean to you. Maybe instead of a gift, you write them a letter, filling the pages of your appreciation for all they have done for you. Thanking them for being understanding when you as a scholar, where at times somewhat abrupt and even rude. Yes, you could make your parents feel that this is a glorious Christmas gift.

The Spirit of Christmas

Then at the same time you as a father or mother could write a letter to your children expressing how much they mean to you.

Each year I wrote to my wife, son and daughter, telling them what joys they had given me during the year. It binds a family love and Christmas then to us had a meaning of love—respect and happiness.

But I was sent the following letter by a radio listener which really expresses love from mother to son.

LETTER FROM A MOTHER TO HER SON

My son,

I have an ache in my heart and a lump in my throat—do you know why? Because I suddenly realized that you are leaving school.

I know you did your best in the examinations and if you perhaps fail, do not be disheartened; try again and then you will succeed. It seems like yesterday that you went to school for the first time, holding my hand so tightly, looking so scared and so very small. Trying so hard not to cry. Did you know that your mother also felt like crying?

Funny, I feel the same way now.

When I look at you now, I feel so proud to call you my son. Your muscular body, fine legs and arrogant stare—a grown man ready to face a new life.

Next year you'll find yourself in a new world—the world of adults. A world full of problems, but also lots of excitement, happiness and kindness. You will meet so many different kinds of people. Beautiful people! But also many with nasty streaks! Please, my son, be patient with those who are unhappy and always make time to listen when they come to you needing an understanding heart. Try to comfort those with heartaches and pray for wisdom to help those who have problems. Be happy about the success of others. Praising them in all sincerity; and real happiness will be your every-day companion.

Remember when competing in life's race, you can always expect a laurel leaf at the end, if you abide by the rules. When perhaps you fail, do not be discouraged—always try again, and learn by your mistakes.

145

Never sacrifice your principles for the sake of being popular—then others will respect and like you for what you are.

Temptation will cross your path, but when in doubt. Do not just tag along, pray for guidance. If perhaps you do fall along the way, take punishment like a man and start again.

Thank you always for being a wonderful son. Forgive the times I had to be strict and maybe sometimes seem unfair. I did what I believed was right, always wanting the most for you and trying to prepare you for the day when you had to spread your wings.

Please treat your elders and seniors with the same respect and good manners.

Whenever you feel unhappy and lonely, remember that someone is always near to you and will keep you if you believe and trust in Him. Never forget to be thankful for everyday blessings.

Always be proud of your home, your school and your country. Give thanks to your teachers, who each and everyone prepared you for your life ahead.

Best of luck for next year and may God bless you and keep you always. With my love.

Mum.

These thoughts which I have shared in this article relating to what Christmas really means, I trust will remind you of the reason we celebrate at this time of year. Jesus wanted us all to love one another regardless of who we are and what mistakes we have made.

To all the readers of "Your Family", may your Christmases be very special to you this year. May you be blessed in your future. May you always be filled with the love you so richly deserve. May the spirit of Jesus prevail in all you do and all you say.

I close by trusting that the spirit of Christmas will be in your heart forever.

22 *Techniques for achieving a happy living*

"I reckon a man can be just about as happy as he makes up his mind to be," said Abraham Lincoln. There is so much truth in these positive words.

MAKE A DAILY RESOLVE

When you awaken each morning and before you get up, say to yourself "I'm going to be happy today."

Expand this idea a little more—"I'm not going to be pessimistic, I'm not going to grumble, I'm not going to criticize. I'm going to be happy instead. I'm going to really try to be loving and understanding. I'm going to enjoy being alive this day. I'm going to be happy."

The habit of declaring what you intend to expect will do wonders in transforming each day. Eventually your whole life style will change. You will find it so effective that you will begin to wonder why you never did it before.

Happiness is a great purger of undesirable emotions. You cannot be happy and jealous, or hateful, or angry at the same time. Happiness cannot live with the undesirable emotions.

If happiness is invited to be our heart's desire, it will take a lot to upset this feeling during the day. So remember, tomorrow morning when you wake up, resolve to be happy!

OUTLAW NEGATIVE THOUGHTS AND EMOTIONS

In spite of the power of happiness, negative thinking and emotions are so prevalent, so contagious and so persistently active, that a special warning is necessary.

First, you must realise that it is possible to be master of your thoughts. For you have only to persist in a certain line of thought, and your emotions will be aroused.

If you would control your emotions, thought control is essential; it is not difficult as is commonly supposed. You can learn to switch off a train of thought as easily as a light.

And almost as easily—if you will—you may plug into positive thoughts, and in that way induce the warmth and comfort of positive emotions like love and joy.

People wallow for years in self-pity or worry or hatred, and all the time they are causing harmful effects to mind and body.

Anyone who doubts this should read Dr John Schindler's book "How to Live 365 Days a Year". I can assure the readers of "Your Family" this is a great book if you can possibly obtain a copy.

Speaking from long experience at the Monroe Clinic, Dr Schindler quotes case after case to prove the theory that negative emotions upset the harmonious working of the body, thus causing a wide range of physical ailments.

While many an invalid with the right mental approach to his or her life's challenge can cope, because of a happy disposition. Those who are basically physically fit should keep it that way, by the right attitude to living. Being fit does not necessarily bring happiness, but surely it has an advantage over constantly feeling out of sorts.

You would do well then to keep yourself fit, not only by taking adequate exercise but also by refusing to entertain such emotions as jealousy, envy, hatred, fear, despair, and pessimism.

MAKE WAR ON WORRY

Worry is faith in reverse. It is the belief or fear that something harmful will either befall ourselves or those we love. This is negative thinking.

If you are a worrier, ask yourself why. It may be you have slipped into this habit without being aware of it. Perhaps one or both or your parents were worriers and you grew up in an atmosphere of worry.

Now determine you need not be a worrier any more.

When you have a problem, the sensible thing is to face it squarely and to think about it positively and constructively.

First determine what has caused the problem. Then consider the various solutions which lie open to you. Finally, decide on what you consider is the best solution and act accordingly.

Ask yourself—"How would I advise a friend in a similar situation?" This will help you to overcome your problem.

SERVE AND MIX WITH OTHERS

One of the best answers for depression is to mix with others—or better still to serve them in some way. We forget our own troubles when we are trying to help others. In many cases our own troubles seem small as we get involved with other people.

149

I am convinced, that when we willingly give service to others it brings a feeling of happiness into our lives.

Mixing with others from time to time is also a way to feel a joy of living and a contentment which has been lacking when we are only thinking of ourselves.

There is generally a spirit or friendship and laughter in the company of others. It is a tonic we all need and certainly it teaches us not to take life too seriously.

HAVE A REASONABLE AMBITION

We all like to feel that we are moving forward towards the attainment of some desirable objective. It is depressing to know we are in a rut.

But if your ambitions are reasonable you will always have a goal to work for.

In Dr Schindlers book he cites the need for new experiences (together with security, affection, creative expression, recognition, and self-esteem), as basic in every person.

It is not so much the new experience itself as the promise of it that does us good. So it is wisdom to have always some distant objective before us to keep alive hope, anticipation and interest.

DON'T EXPECT PERFECTION OR GRATITUDE

Perfection is only something we strive for and never quite reach. Gratitude we should not expect, if we do we will so often be disappointed, for praise and thanks is something that at times is missing in the modern world.

If you give a service because this is what you want to

do,then gratitude is not necessary, although it is appreci- ated when given. Otherwise you can become, bitter and upset and believe no one cares about what you do for them. Leaving the way to unhappiness and maybe indifference. Causing as you know only too well emotional and negative thinking.

PROVIDE FOR YOUR OWN BASIC NEEDS

It is doubtful if anyone is truly happy if the majority of the person's basic needs are not provided for in some way. Let me list a few:

(1) To have food and bodily comfort.
(2) To love and be loved.
(3) To feel useful and needed.
(4) To create or construct something.
(5) To protect the weak and helpless.
(6) To find out—to be curious.
(7) To be understanding and understood.
(8) To escape from danger.
(9) To gain, possess, acquire.
(10) To laugh.
(11) To repel unpleasantness.
(12) To be able to appeal for help and receive it.
(13) To mix with others.
(14) To do a job of work that gives satisfaction.

I am sure you can add many more to this list, but trust they can throw some light on our desires.

Our work, leisure, and way of life must make some

151

provision for at least most of the above. Naturally, the strength of these needs varies with the individual, and this accounts for the varied attitude of human behaviour.

A careful inspection will show you which instincts you have which are stronger than others.

If you are mentally curious and your job is too routine and unsatisfying, you had better take up seriously some part-time study which will give you some feeling of accomplishment.

To some the only way to reach a target or goal is to be creative. Such hobbies are painting, building, constructing or writing.

Others find joining a club or society will bring out their best especially if they hold a position which others look upon as one of leadership.

So by enlightened understanding of your nature and a wise controlling of your life, you will undoubtedly induce a large measure of constant happiness.

APPRECIATE WHAT YOU HAVE

Although we must keep a reasonable ambition in front of ourselves, we should also remain appreciative of the many good things we already possess.

Good health should be a constant source of thankfulness and appreciation.

Then there are many blessings we should hold in mind: (a) employment, (b) happy family life, (c) friendships, (d) a comfortable home.

Never lose sight of all that you have and have achieved. Keep a happy eye and especially a happy heart on your loved ones. Count your blessings when you are loved by others.

There's a very special saying which I have found most enlightening:

"As you amble along through life, brother, no matter what's your goal, keep your eye upon the doughnut and not upon the hole."

23 *Increase your personal charm*

Charm is a quality which covers a multitude of shortcomings. You may not be brilliant or attractive, but if you have charm you will be accepted and popular.

Some are naturally charming, others have to develop it. How do you stand?

Perhaps we had better try to define charm. It is certainly not an insincere attitude to others. Some people are at times suspicious of the word charm—because it could mean show-off.

So let us define charm this way: "A combination of qualities and characteristics which are generally found pleasing."

If you don't know whether others find you charming, ask yourself the following questions:

How's my appearance.

Your mirror doesn't flatter you? Don't worry: good looks do not enter into charm. Some of the world's most charming people are often called ugly.

To most people, though, your general rather than social appearance does matter.

Is my voice attractive

Do you speak attractively or do you growl or mumble. Do you rush your words. Do you speak too softly, so that others have to interrupt you, because they couldn't hear you?

If you have to remedy any of these faults, do so and you will certainly increase your charm.

154

Increase your personal charm

Do I smile readily?

You will never be known as charming until you learn to smile easily.

Have you ever thought a glum looking person was charming? Notice how a smile improves the appearance of someone you know. People look much younger when they smile. Please try it yourself!

Don't you feel more relaxed and confident when you smile? Smiling is good for your nerves and it will help improve your health. As far as work is concerned you'll do a much tougher job if it is done with a smile.

Smiling helps others to like you. It breaks down prejudices, overcomes resentment and reserve and increases our friendships.

Get into the habit of smiling easily as soon as possible.

Am I an optimist?

Have you ever heard of a pessimist being renowned for his or her charm? Somehow charm and pessimism don't go together.

To become an optimist practice control of your thoughts and your spoken word. Do all you can to stop imagining the worst.

Avoid self pity at all costs. Cancel your subscription to the P.L.O.M. Club. "The Poor Little Old Me, Club."

Thinking cheerful thoughts will surely increase your charm.

Am I thoughtful of others?

Consideration is an essential ingredient of charm.

Ask yourself whether you think sufficiently of the feelings, welfare and comfort of others.

155

If you feel you've been remiss here, why not resolve to be more thoughtful in the future?

Old habits are best overcome by new ones, but as they require a little effort at first, resolve to do at least one unselfish action each day.

Remember that all of us are sensitive to what others feel about us.

Kindness, tact, unselfishness, modesty—these are the ingredients of charm. They spring from thoughtfulness.

Do I show appreciation?

Are you quick to express appreciation? Are you generous with praise? Are you grateful for the things people do for you?

When you thank people for something, say it with feeling, all of us like to be appreciated.

Do not forget that if you are married with a family, the children like to be appreciated as well. Also children have to show appreciation to their parents.

Am I a good conversationalist?

You must be ready to join in conversations. If you find this difficult at first, learn to be a good listener. Give people your full attention as they speak to you. So often we appear to be disinterested! Reading current affairs is a help to get you started. By this method you are ready to express your own views during a discussion with friends.

How are my manners?

Can you imagine a charming person conducting himself in a rude manner. In these modern times, manners are sometimes forgotten. Yet they play a vital role in our lives.

Increase your personal charm

We are so often misunderstood due to our bad manners, when underneath people are kind and considerate. We are taken at the way we behave. Courtesy is so important and it can open many doors to our future. Not that courtesy is "put on", but rather is it part of the persons nature. Children learn from parents how to conduct themselves, and so often we express our thanks to the young when they are courteous to older people.

Manners do play a key role in the way we live and it is good at times to take a look at our daily behaviour. Namely as we drive our cars! In answering the telephone!

Good manners equals charm in action.

Do I have self-confidence?

True self-confidence, at which we should aim may be identified as follows:

We have to know our strengths and weaknesses. We must not allow the weaknesses to cloud our vision of what we have achieved. To begin to appreciate our own abilities is a step in the direction of being true to ourselves. This brings out the truth that all people including ourselves are important people.

The truly self-confident persons have come to terms with reality. So they know they can make mistakes and not pull themselves down. They become self-assured when they realise that others who have achieved vast successes, have at one time failed at something, before striking the right goal.

The persons who lack self-confidence often find it difficult to work with others. Thus they stifle their real personality, and never allow their true charm to show itself.

The people who have essential self-confidence can work well with others. They can be objective about a task to be done.

The reasonableness, co-operative spirit and gentle manners to be found in nearly all truly self-confident people all spring from an inner security. Once we have accepted ourselves and are living more or less at peace with ourselves our charm blossoms forth.

Do I encourage others?

Although it is not the most important part of your life to have people thinking well of you, for first of all you have to think well of yourself. It is a reassuring fact that to have others thinking highly of you does make your life a lot easier to cope with. A certain way to experience this, is to encourage others as much as possible.

When you encourage a person he feels needed and also becomes excited about himself. You will have helped someone on a path of happiness. At the same time you have probably added to his self-esteem. Also by encouragement they will continue in some direction to obtain their goal.

We are all thirsty for the approval of our fellows. That is why encouragement works wonders. It has made strong men out of weaklings, millionaires out of newspaper-boys.

It has changed lives, healed broken hearts, rekindled hope, mended marriages that had been on the rocks, and saved many from suicides.

The giving of encouragement costs you nothing beyond thoughtfulness and a little time. It can take the form of a scribbled note, a card, an apparently casual remark, a nod, a handshake, a hug.

Children and young people easily get discouraged. A helping hand, an interested inquiry, a reminder of rewards ahead. A reference to something already achieved—any of these will encourage them on their way. If you have children or meet children in anyway, give out encouragement freely.

If you employ others or are in charge of them, remember that encouragement acts like a lubricant. It always results in better and more willing service. Who doesn't think the boss is great or charming when he has received a word of praise from him?

There is too little praise or encouragement around these days, so let each one of us, add a little more pleasure and enjoyment in the lives of those around us.

In conclusion if you wish to increase your personal charm remember it is a combination of qualities and characteristics which others find pleasing and you feel at peace with yourself, by liking what you do.

Increase your charm by asking yourself the following questions.

How's my appearance? Is my voice attractive? Do I smile readily? Am I an optimist? Am I thoughtful of others? Do I show appreciation? Am I a good conversationalist? How are my manners? Do I have self-confidence? Do I encourage others?

Work on yourself until you are able to give an unqualified positive answer to all the above questions—and then charming indeed you will be!

24 *Your Struggle to overcome resentment*

I have lectured to many thousands of people—so different in many ways, and yet all wanting to make something of their lives. About finding themselves, about achieving happiness and fulfilment. Self esteem is the key to human dignity.

But in seeking to express self-esteem, you have to do more than believe in a positive mental attitude: You must develop the capacity to overcome negative destructive tendencies. One of these is resentment.

I have written previously about the inferiority complex, but now let us consider the resentment complex.

Let me spell it out:

1. Revenge
2. Envy
3. Sulkiness
4. Exception
5. Nasty
6. Temper
7. Misery
8. Enmity
9. Neglect
10. Tension

See how the above causes people to be unhappy and how it stops them from finding their true path in life.

1. *Revenge*

You feel you have been wronged. A victim of injustice. So

inwardly you now seek revenge. But who do you hurt: only yourself. You find it affects the nerves. You do not eat well. You find it disturbs your sleep. The obsession for getting your own back causes you untold harm.

2. *Envy*

Another feeling you can do without. When you envy someone else, you are in fact seeing yourself being inferior to the other person. Stop envying anyone else, but begin to admire your own talents and build a better self-image.

3. *Sulkiness*

You find people appear not to notice you or even accept your advice. You say you won't have any further contact with this type of person so you switch off and sulk. This develops eventually into a resentment pattern against life itself. The alternative, take people as they are and know the only person you can change is yourself.

4. *Exception*

You may find yourself taking great exception to what others say. You begin to resent anything that looks like a form of criticism against yourself. So again realise that we are not all alike. Reject the idea that everyone is against you and accept people as they are. Don't let criticism hurt you, but maybe you can learn from it.

5. *Nasty*

When you resent a person, you can become nasty towards them. In fact you can find fault with nearly everything they say or do. A changed attitude is needed.

161

Try and see some good in a person and eventually we are no longer unpleasant.

6. *Temper*

Temper is the explosive reaction to frustration. This is because people who lose their tempers over small things are unable to express themselves in a normal way. Then they become frustrated with themselves and lose control over their actions. All need to learn the art of having a quiet time each day. Thus bringing about more tranquility in all they do.

7. *Misery*

Resentment brings misery into many lives. You see around you so much unhappiness caused by people who resent others. They allow hurts to make them miserable, not seeing the good things in their lives.

Watch your reaction to situations which seem to bring resentment in your attitude to others.

Only by controlling your thoughts can you begin to throw off these challenging situations which come to all at sometime or another.

8. *Enmity*

Many create a hostile world about them. All people appear to be unfriendly and unco-operative to the person who feels let down. This is why you have to carefully look at your own response to people. Are you friendly? Or are you basically hostile?

9. *Neglect*

Do you at times feel neglected? Maybe if you are married

you think quite rightly that your partner is not taking as much notice of you as he should. Then how do you deal with this situation. Sulk—hit back or do you check to see if you have neglected your husband or wife as the case may be.

Resentment soon shows its unpleasant head and unless you immediately correct this inner feeling, happiness disappears and the joys of marriage have gone.

Yes! We all think we are neglected at certain times. So talk it out and communicate with loving thoughts.

10. *Tension*

When resentment becomes a habit, so does tension. For resentment and tension are twins—not identical, but twins nonetheless.

The resentment complex is a composite of negative forces; of revenge, envy, negligence and narrow-mindedness. The total result brings with it tension.

You do not need these unpleasant thoughts—so once more learn to relax and shake off the killer which is tension. For it plays havoc mentally and physically.

So now let us plan a positive approach towards resentment. To find self-respect, you must find in yourself the weapon to use against the negation of resentment.

First, you must know you are not alone when you feel resentment. Everyone feels resentful sometimes, because everyone, at one time or another, experiences frustration, grief, disappointment and despair. The distinction is this: The person who lacks self-respect stays resentful, fails to get over it, inflicts his hostility on others; the person with self-respect climbs out of the pit, gets over it, goes on to a constructive life of which he or she can be proud.

Living your life*Living your life*

An example of how we can resent someone, even though we love the other, is the following story of a married couple who came to me for help.

Mary and John had been married for some 15 years. During this time three children were born. All on the surface seemed to be a happy story of family life. Now something seemed to trigger off the feeling of resentment Mary had against John. During early married life Mary and John did most things together, planning a home, annual holidays and sometimes weekends away. But Mary fell pregnant and so as time moved on the two were unable to go away so much. Mary had to give up her job, when the arrival of the first child was due. John at first did his best to help his wife, by doing little extra things about the house. Getting the shopping was his assistance on Saturday mornings. But John got quick promotion and spent longer periods at the office and now because he was an executive he was expected to play golf on Saturday mornings. Yes! Because his salary had increased they were able to employ a servant to assist Mary at home. Unfortunately neither John nor Mary were really aware of what was taking place in their lives. Mary was seeing less of John than before and in addition the arrival of baby number two. John because of his business commitments spent little time with his wife and children. Mary quite happy to tend to the children and look after her man. Then baby number three was born and Mary had her hands full with three children to bring up.

Then came the day when Mary was talking to some of her friends about married life. For the first time she became aware of her frustrations as friend after friend told her not to go on being a slave in the home. Resentment which no doubt was building up within Mary exploded. Whilst

164

waiting for John to come home she sat down and thought out what had taken place in their 15 years of marriage. At first bliss and then bound to a family which didn't appreciate her. Husband away on business trips, she left alone to cope. Annual holidays still looking after the children— really no holiday.

When John arrived home that night tired and irritable he was met with an enraged wife telling him she had had enough and wanted out. No amount of reasoning helped and finally he too became angry. Words were said by both to each other so unkindly that divorce was the only answer.

During their visits to me, hoping to find a suitable solution because of the children, both for the first time opened up and expressed their feelings about each other.

Mary said "She felt imprisoned in the home" and couldn't understand why she had accepted it for so long. John on the other hand could not appreciate what all the fuss was about, as surely while "I earn the living, she should be able to look after the children and the home" adding "willingly".

Resentment is so ugly, that love seems to depart and hurt, frustrations and fears takes its place.

Here we have two normal reasonably adjusted people when they first married now behaving as though they were strangers.

What had gone wrong? Neither had sat down and talked about (a) What would happen when the first baby was born, how would it effect their lives. (b) No discussion as to what would be expected of John after promotion. In other words no communication, no planning.

Nothing takes care of itself, planning, adjusting, under-

16

standing, tolerance had to be discussed—talked over and talked out.

Let me summarize this advice.

(1) Rise above any thoughts of resentment—be it what has happened to you in the past. Get rid of any self-pity.
(2) Set daily goals: You are worth it. Stop turning your resentment in on yourself. Move towards your goals instead.
(3) Forgive others—at least try. Remember no one is perfect. Forgiveness takes away resentment.
(4) Forgive yourself no matter what you have done in the past. It is hard I know—but work at this key to happiness.